Weetabix

Book of the
MILLENNIUM

Volume 2: 1351–1700

from the publishers of
The **HUTCHINSON**
ENCYCLOPEDIA

Helicon

First published for Weetabix Limited in Great Britain in 1999 by
Helicon Publishing Ltd
42 Hythe Bridge Street
Oxford OX1 2EP
e-mail address: admin@helicon.co.uk
Web site: http://www.helicon.co.uk

The Weetabix name and logo are the registered trade marks of Weetabix Limited.

Typesetting by Tech Type, Abingdon, Oxon
Layout and design by Norton Matrix Limited, Bath
Printed in Italy by De Agostini, Novara
ISBN: 1-85986-326-4

British Library Cataloguing in Publication Data

A catalogue record for this book is available from the British Library.

Papers used by Helicon Publishing Ltd are natural recyclable products
made from wood grown in sustainable forests. The manufacturing
processes of both raw material and paper conform to the environmental
regulations of the country of origin.

Contributors and Advisors

Ian Crofton   Susan Mendelsohn

Bernadette Crowley   Nigel Seaton

Susan Cuthbert   Cath Senker

Giles Hastings   Andrew Solway

Maggy Hendry   Lisa Sullivan

Louise Jones   Sarah Wearne

Brenda Lofthouse   Christine Withers

Editorial and Production

Editorial Director   **Production**
Hilary McGlynn   Tony Ballsdon

Managing Editor   **Picture Research**
Katie Emblen   Elizabeth Loving

Project Managers   **Cartography**
Robert Snedden   Olive Pearson
Lisa Sullivan

                             Art and Design
                             Terence Caven
Editors
Rachel Minay
Edith Summerhayes

Contents

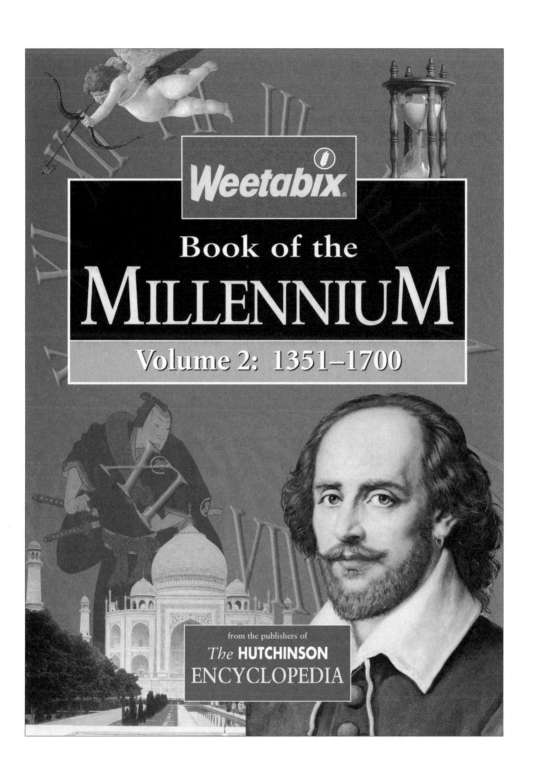

Weetabix

Book of the
MILLENNIUM

Volume 2: 1351–1700

from the publishers of
The **HUTCHINSON**
ENCYCLOPEDIA

The World 1351–1700

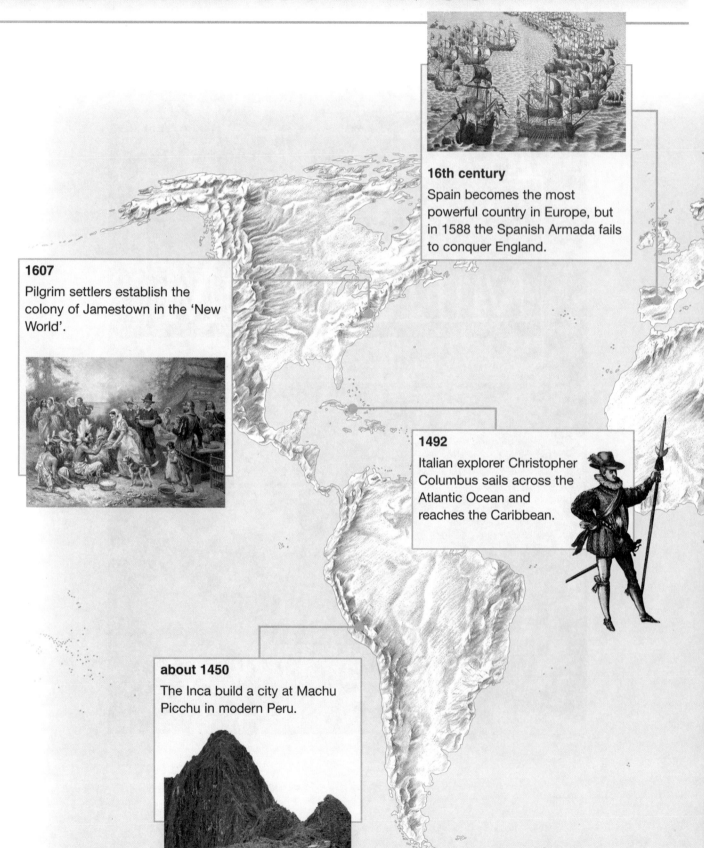

16th century

Spain becomes the most powerful country in Europe, but in 1588 the Spanish Armada fails to conquer England.

1607

Pilgrim settlers establish the colony of Jamestown in the 'New World'.

1492

Italian explorer Christopher Columbus sails across the Atlantic Ocean and reaches the Caribbean.

about 1450

The Inca build a city at Machu Picchu in modern Peru.

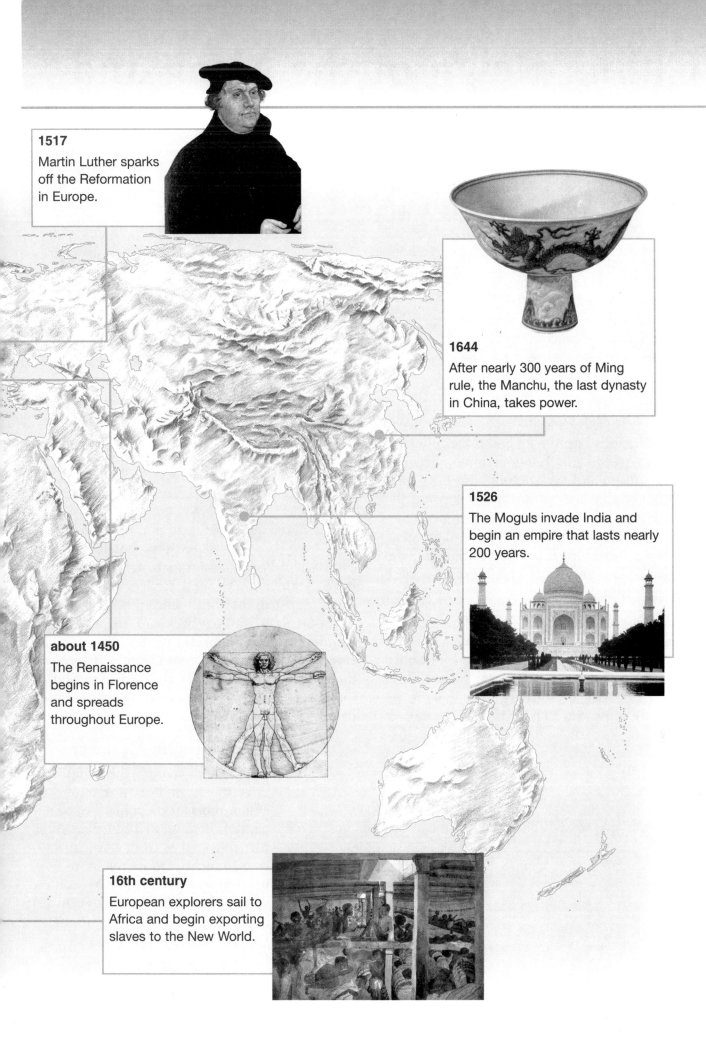

1517

Martin Luther sparks off the Reformation in Europe.

1644

After nearly 300 years of Ming rule, the Manchu, the last dynasty in China, takes power.

1526

The Moguls invade India and begin an empire that lasts nearly 200 years.

about 1450

The Renaissance begins in Florence and spreads throughout Europe.

16th century

European explorers sail to Africa and begin exporting slaves to the New World.

China: Reign of the Ming and Manchu

The Ming Dynasty

For almost 100 years the Mongols, people from Mongolia, ruled China. Then, in 1368 Chinese rebels drove out the Mongols and a native Chinese Buddhist monk became the new emperor. He called himself Hong Wu and established the Ming Dynasty (line of emperors), which ruled China for nearly 300 years.

Ming China was very stable. The emperor made all the decisions because he had direct power over the government. The government became very organized and less corrupt, and the basic structure established by the Ming lasted until 1912. For many years the country enjoyed peace and prosperity, and it expanded greatly, extending north into Korea and Mongolia, west into Turkestan, and south into Vietnam and Myanmar (Burma).

In the early 15th century a Chinese admiral, Zheng He, set out on a series of voyages of trade and discovery, reaching the Spice Islands (the Moluccas in Indonesia), Arabia, and the east coast of Africa. However, after this the Chinese began to turn inwards, and the next

The delicately painted porcelain of the Ming Dynasty is thought to be among the most beautiful ever produced.

important contact with the outside world came when Portuguese traders arrived in China in the 16th century. These traders set up a trading post in the south, and took Chinese silk, porcelain, and tea back to Europe. This contact was not important to the Ming emperors, however, because they saw China as the centre of the world. In the mid-16th century the government banned any voyages by Chinese people outside China.

The Manchu Dynasty

By the 17th century the Ming government had become weaker. When rebels took control of the capital, Beijing, in 1644, the Ming turned to tribes from Manchuria (the Manchus) to help restore government power. The Manchus seized power for themselves instead and established the Manchu, or Qing dynasty, which ruled China for nearly 300 years.

At first the Manchus thought they were superior to the Chinese and rejected their culture, but gradually

MANCHURIA

CHINA Beijing

Macao

——— Ming China in 1368

▨ Manchu homeland

▨ Manchu China

Since 1949 the Forbidden City has been open to the public as a museum.

The Forbidden City

The Forbidden City was a giant palace built in 1421 in Beijing by Yung Lo, the third Ming emperor. It contained various grand houses, temples, and parks. It was called the Forbidden City because no ordinary citizens and no foreigners at all were allowed inside its walls. The Forbidden City became a sacred place and a symbol of the great power of the Chinese emperors.

Hong Wu (ruled 1368–1398)

Hong Wu was born a peasant in 1328. In his early life he was a Buddhist monk who earned his living by begging. Later he became a leader of rebels against the Mongol rulers. In 1368 he founded the Ming dynasty after a revolt drove out the last Mongol emperor. He was the first Chinese emperor in more than 1,000 years to come from a peasant background.

Perhaps because of his background, Hong Wu went out of his way to help the poor. He abolished slavery, imposed heavy taxes on the rich, took land away from the big landowners and gave it to the poor, and encouraged primary education throughout his empire. Hong Wu also strengthened the army, and he and later Ming rulers extended the Chinese empire more than any native rulers had done before. Towards the end of his rule Hong Wu began to take more and more power himself, not trusting advisors and other government officials. He died in 1398.

they adopted Chinese ways. China continued to flourish under the Manchus. The empire grew to three times its size, and the government became more orderly and efficient. European thinkers in the 18th century such as Voltaire wrote about how much they admired the Chinese system of government. The Manchus continued to produce silk and porcelain and to trade with Europeans. However, although the Manchus exported their goods to Europe and America, they did not allow many European imports into the country, so that China would not be too influenced by the West. This policy caused China to become isolated and to lose a lot of its wealth. The Manchu dynasty began to weaken in the 19th century. It was the last of the Chinese dynasties, and was replaced by a republic at the beginning of the 20th century.

Japan: *Samurai* and *Shoguns*

In the 8th century the emperor of Japan divided the country between members of his family. These new landowners, who remained in the royal palace, appointed barons, called *daimyo*, to run the estates for them. Farmers and craftsmen worked on the estates, and warriors called *samurai* kept order. Rival *daimyos* often fought each other for land, power, and honour.

Within a few centuries, some *daimyo* had become more powerful than the emperor. At the end of the 12th century a daimyo called Yoritomo Minamoto had become the most powerful man in Japan. In 1192 the emperor gave him the title *shogun*, which means 'great general'. Although the emperor still officially ruled Japan, the *shogun* was the country's real ruler. *Shoguns* stayed in power for almost 700 years, until a revolution took place in 1867, when the *shogun* was overthrown and an emperor once again became ruler.

Under the *shoguns*, Japanese society was divided into four categories. At the top were the *daimyo*, the royal family, and the *samurai*.

A portrait of a mounted *samurai*. *Samurai* were the equivalent of European knights.

Young *Samurai*

Young *samurai* went to school and were taught many subjects. The most important were the two basic skills of warfare – how to kill and how to survive. Students spent many years practising sword fighting, hand-to-hand combat, and archery. When guns arrived in Japan in the 15th century, students also learned how to use them. Between the ages of 13 and 15 young *samurai* officially became adults. They received weapons and a suit of armour, and were given a *samurai* hairstyle, where the hair was shaved at the front and tied in a ponytail at the back.

The armour worn by a *samurai*.

The second category contained the farmers, who had the important job of growing the country's food. The third category contained craftsmen. The lowest category included traders, since they did not make anything but brought and sold the work of others.

Samurai warriors came from *samurai* families, and a boy could not become a *samurai* unless he was born or adopted into one of these families. *Samurai* followed a code of conduct known as *bushido,* which means 'way of the warrior'. It taught *samurai* to place fearlessness, self-sacrifice, loyalty, and honour above life itself. Facing dishonour or defeat, a *samurai* committed suicide by *seppuku* (also called *hara-kiri*), a ritual where he slit open his stomach. From the 12th century the *samurai* adopted a religion called Zen Buddhism. It taught its followers to clear the mind of worry and fear.

A collection of armour and weapons used by a *samurai*.

The Tokugawa Shogunate

In the 16th century Japan was ravaged by civil war, as the *daimyos* fought each other for power. The Ashikaga family had become *shoguns* in the 14th century, but had lost control of the country long before they finally lost their power in 1578. Towards the end of the 16th century three great military leaders in turn managed to fight their way to supreme power in Japan. The last of these, Tokugawa Ieyasu, made himself *shogun* in 1603, and his family continued to rule until 1868. The Tokugawa *shoguns* moved the capital from Kyoto to Edo (now called Tokyo). They also reduced the power of the *daimyos* and *samurai*, and restored order and stability to Japan.

Foreign Visitors

In the 1540s Portuguese traders became the first Europeans to land in Japan. They were closely followed by other traders, who brought guns to Japan for the first time. A few years later, Christian missionaries arrived to try to convert the Japanese to Christianity. In 1633 the *shogun* Tokugawa Iemitsu, fearing the growing foreign influence, decreed that all foreigners should be banned from Japan and no Japanese were to travel abroad. Christianity was also banned, and Japanese Christians were forced to convert to the Buddhist religion. This period of isolation from the outside world was to last for over 200 years.

Arts from the Orient

For thousands of years, the cultures of China and Japan developed in complete isolation from the West. The Chinese began selling their silk and porcelain to European traders, but took only gold or silver in exchange. They did not want Western goods. For over 200 years, Japanese people were not allowed to travel outside the country and no foreigners were allowed in. Because of this, Chinese and Japanese art is very different from European art.

Chinese Art

The Ming dynasty (line of emperors) ruled China from 1368 to 1644. At first, it lived up to its name, which means 'bright' or 'brilliant'. Many artists and craftsmen were busy with great projects for the emperor's court, including splendid buildings in the Forbidden City of Beijing. Long scrolls were painted of endless journeys through constantly changing landscapes. A kind of enamelware called cloisonné, which came to China from Byzantium, decorated metal vases and bowls. Carpets, carvings, lacquerware, and magnificent embroidered silk robes

Women have been banned from the stage in Japan since 1629 and only men perform in Japanese theatre.

Japanese Theatre

No drama first appeared around the 14th century. It is one of the oldest theatrical forms in the world. *No* means 'skill' in Japanese. *No* plays are performed by male actors on an almost empty stage. It is very religious in nature and the main character is usually a god or a demon. A *No* play is usually quite short. Traditionally a series of three *No* plays are performed together in a programme that lasts all day. In between the serious *No* plays there are more light-hearted Kyogen plays, which tell funny stories.

Kabuki theatre became popular in Japan from about 1600. It combines singing, dancing, mime, and spectacular staging. The actors wear dazzling costumes and carved masks, and the main character often changes his costume to reveal his true identity at the end of the play. Red, white, and black make-up adds to the dramatic effect. There are two main kinds of *Kabuki* play: *jidaimono*, or pseudo-historical pieces, and *sewamono*, or stories dealing with Japanese cultural life. There are also modern plays. *Kabuki* theatre takes many of its ideas from the older No plays. Like No drama, a *Kabuki* play lasts all day and gives audiences a variety of play styles and acting.

also showed the skills of Ming craftspeople.

Potters made delicate vases from very fine white clay called porcelain, which began to be called china in the Western world. Some vases were as thin as an eggshell, with blue and white glazes. European traders came to China for the first time to buy these Ming vases.

Other artists broke away from the court and started a new experimental style of painting, done by flinging ink onto the paper. Their pictures look more rough and careless, but were actually done very skilfully.

A pair of bronze lion dogs made during the Ming dynasty.

A beautiful Chinese necklace of gold, silver, pearls, coral, and kingfisher feathers, probably made to mark a special occasion.

Japanese Art

When the Ashikaga family came to rule Japan in 1392, there had been 50 years of civil war, and many temples filled with art works had been burned down. Soon, under the influence of the Ashikagas, people started to collect and copy fine Chinese art. Beautiful folding screens were painted, with misty poetic scenes in black and white. Japanese painting is inspired by Zen Buddhism, a popular religion in Japan, so the ink is used in a disciplined and quiet, but bold, way. The main subject is often off-centre, and empty space in the painting is important to the picture.

From the middle of the 16th century bright new screens and sliding panels were created to decorate the grand castles of the warrior class. Rich and gorgeous colours were painted on a gold or silver background. Beautiful pottery and lacquerware were also designed during this time. Some artists were famous for their elegant calligraphy (handwriting), painted with brush and ink. Soon, however, Japan stopped trading with merchants from the outside world. The government did not want foreigners to influence Japan.

Africa: Challenge to the Coasts

Africa in the Middle Ages was rich in natural resources. Copper and iron were mined in central Africa, and there were salt lakes on the western coast. African textiles were in great demand for their rich colours and fine quality. The kingdoms of West Africa and Zimbabwe were very rich in gold.

An African ceremonial mask.

A blacksmith forging iron in west central Africa. This man's ancestors may well have been Songhai.

Masks

In many African societies, the use of masks was a vital part of life. Their use involves the belief that a mask has its own identity, which enters the body and mind of the wearer. People thought that masks could bring gods, spirits, animals, and dead relatives to life.

Islam was firmly established in North Africa, and Arab traders continued to spread its influence to the south. They established trading posts on the East African coast, which grew more and more prosperous. They were taking goods from inside

Elmina Castle in Ghana, built by the Portuguese as a base for slave trading.

Africa and selling them in Asia and the Middle East. Trade routes ran from North Africa south through the Sahara Desert to West Africa.

In the 15th century Portuguese explorers and merchants arrived on the western coast, and began trading for gold. By the end of the century Spain was challenging their domination of the African gold trade, and other Europeans had started to trade all along the coast of Africa south of the Sahara. The slave trade was firmly established, and the Dutch also began to compete with the Portuguese.

The Songhai Empire

In 1350 the Songhai people, whose kingdom was in the region of Gao, were under the rule of the great empire of Mali. They were wealthy and strong. In the late 15th century, under the ruler Sonni Ali, the influence of the Songhai spread. Soon their power far exceeded that of Mali. They controlled the trade routes across the Sahara, the great trading cities of Jenne and Timbuktu, and the area westwards to Senegal. By 1582 the empire extended as far as Cameroon.

In 1591 Moroccan forces attacked the Songhai, taking several cities. By 1618 the Moroccans had gained control of most of the empire. They never completely overthrew the Songhai, however. Even today, Songhai peoples control much of the Saharan caravan trade.

Sonni Ali (ruled about 1464–1492)

Sonni Ali greatly expanded the Songhai empire, but he was a cruel and ruthless leader in many ways. In 1468 Muslim leaders of Timbuktu asked him to help them overthrow the Tuareg, a nomadic (wandering) tribe that had conquered the city. He drove the Tuareg away, but then captured the city himself and murdered many of the people who lived there. A historian from the 16th century wrote that when someone displeased Sonni Ali, whether a friend or an enemy, that person would often be swiftly killed.

The Slave Trade

Slaves have been sent from Africa to the Mediterranean and the Middle East since ancient times. Massive growth in this trade started in the 15th century, when Europeans began to buy and sell African people as slaves. At first, most people sold in this way were prisoners of war, taken by one African kingdom from another. As the trade grew, Europeans would even seize Africans who were leading peaceful lives, and take them to sell. They knew many Africans were gentle and unsuspecting, and therefore easy to capture. Most African slaves were taken to the Americas, where the plantation system of agriculture relied on the use of unpaid workers who could be worked to the point of exhaustion. The wealth created by the slave trade and slave labour contributed to the economic success of several European and American countries. By 1700 the Dutch, French, British, Danish, and Swedish had joined the Portuguese in the slave trade.

The Ottoman Empire

At the end of the 13th century various Turkish peoples were living in Anatolia (modern Turkey). The Turks were originally nomads, wandering peoples from the grasslands of central Asia. They were Muslims, and were constantly fighting the Christian Byzantine Empire for territory. One of these Turkish groups, led by a warrior named Osman, was stronger than the others. This group, which became known as the Osmani, or Ottomans, after their leader, began to make an empire by taking territory from the Byzantines.

The End of the Byzantine Empire

When the Roman Empire split in two in the 4th century AD the eastern half became the Byzantine Empire. At its height the Byzantine Empire was one of the greatest in history, but by the late 13th century it had lost much of its might and territory. After Osman died his successors continued to fight the Byzantine Empire, taking land in southeastern Europe, including Montenegro, Albania, Bulgaria, Bosnia, part of Greece, and most of Serbia.

In 1453 the Ottoman ruler Sultan Mehmed II led an attack on Constantinople (modern Istanbul), the Byzantine capital. After a long siege, the Turks got into the city and for three days massacred its inhabitants and pillaged its treasures. The last Byzantine emperor, Constantine XI, died defending the city, and its capture by the Turks marked the end of the Byzantine Empire.

Constantinople

After the capture of Constantinople, Mehmed II gained tremendous glory and prestige among his people. He wished to turn the city, which became known as Istanbul, into a capital worthy of the Ottoman Empire. Most of the Christian population had either been massacred or had fled the city, so Mehmed had to get people to live in his new capital. He forced Muslims and Christians from other parts of his empire to move to Istanbul. The city gradually became a thriving metropolis, and within 50 years had become the largest city in Europe.

Ottoman Arts and Sciences

Suleiman I greatly encouraged the arts and sciences, and under his rule the Ottomans produced excellent examples of literature, art, and architecture. Under his direction mosques, bridges, and other public works were built in major cities of the Islamic world. The designs of the great Ottoman architect Sinan were copied by architects of later important Turkish buildings. One of Sinan's most magnificent works is a mosque built for Suleiman in Istanbul. There were some brilliant artists and writers in Suleiman's court, including the famous Turkish poet Baki, whose best work was a poem written for Suleiman when he died.

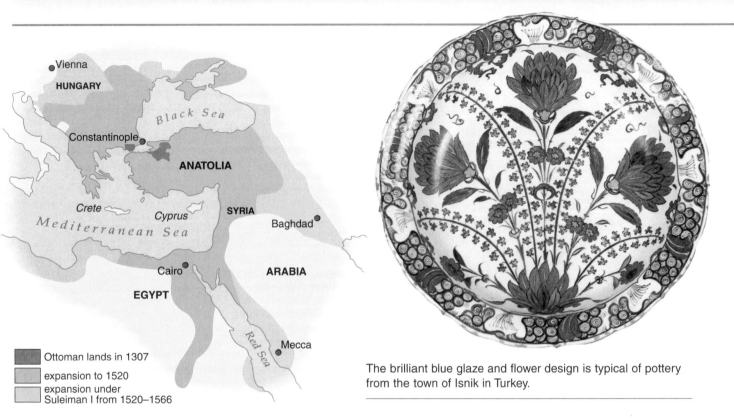

The brilliant blue glaze and flower design is typical of pottery from the town of Isnik in Turkey.

Map legend:
- Ottoman lands in 1307
- expansion to 1520
- expansion under Suleiman I from 1520–1566

Map labels: Vienna, HUNGARY, Black Sea, Constantinople, ANATOLIA, Crete, Cyprus, SYRIA, Baghdad, Mediterranean Sea, Cairo, ARABIA, EGYPT, Red Sea, Mecca

Selim and Suleiman

The Ottoman Empire reached its height from 1512 to 1566 under Sultan Selim I and his son, Suleiman I. Selim conquered Syria, Arabia, and Egypt, while Suleiman added Mesopotamia (modern Iraq), Hungary, and more of North Africa to his empire. He went even further into Europe, to the gates of Vienna, before bad weather and disease forced him to retreat. The Ottomans were now the rulers of most of the Muslim world. Suleiman also made the Ottomans the supreme force in the Mediterranean Sea, giving them control of the valuable trade from the Far East to Europe.

In the late 16th century, after Suleiman died, the Ottoman Empire began to get weaker.

Internal fighting within the empire was the main reason, although military defeats against enemies such as Austria and Russia in the 18th century also hastened the decline. The Ottoman Empire was finally occupied and broken up by the victorious Allies at the end of the First World War in 1918.

Suleiman I (ruled 1520–1566)

The greatest of the sultans, Suleiman I directed daring military campaigns that increased his empire's power and splendour to new heights. In Europe he became known as 'Suleiman the Magnificent'. Among his own people he was called 'the Lawgiver', because he changed the Ottoman legal and tax systems, making them fairer. Suleiman could be very harsh – he ordered the execution of two of his own sons, believing them to be disloyal. For most of his life he focused on his military campaigns, and died while besieging a fortress in Hungary.

Suleiman the Magnificent, sultan of the Ottoman Empire at the height of its powers.

The Empire of the Aztecs

The Aztecs were a nomadic (wandering) people who left northern Mexico to settle in the valley of central Mexico in the 12th century. The Aztecs created a powerful state and a huge capital, Tenochtitlán, built on islands in the middle of Lake Texcoco. The success of the Aztecs was based on their remarkable system of agriculture. They built terraces and irrigation channels on the surrounding hills, and even grew crops on floating rafts in the lake.

The Aztecs were a warlike people, and from the 15th century they began to expand their territory. They conquered hundreds of small neighbouring states, and by the early 16th century had created an empire that covered much of central Mexico. The most important people in Aztec society after the emperor were the warriors. Priests and officials were also important. Beneath them were craftsmen, and then peasants and servants. At the bottom of society were the slaves.

Human sacrifice was an important part of Aztec religion. Slaves were often bought just to be sacrificed to the gods,

This rattlesnake sculpture was made by an Aztec artist in the early 15th century.

and the Aztecs also sacrificed people captured in battle. Noblemen also thought that it was an honour to be sacrificed. Sacrifices took place on the top of the great pyramid-temples, where the chief priest cut the victim's heart out with a stone dagger while the victim was still alive. The number of sacrifices seems to have increased during the 15th century. When the great pyramid of Tenochtitlán was completed in 1489 up to 20,000 people may have been sacrificed.

End of the Empire

The Aztecs were constantly at war to capture more people to sacrifice. They either fought their neighbours, or crushed revolts within their empire. So when the Spanish arrived in Mexico in 1519 they found many peoples willing to help them defeat the Aztecs.

The Spanish conquistadors (conquerors) were led by Hernán Cortés. Representatives of the Aztec emperor Motecuhzoma II (known as Montezuma) gave Cortés gifts of gold to persuade him to go home. But the thought of more gold only made Cortés more determined to conquer the Aztecs. He commanded fewer than 1,000 men, against the Aztec army of 250,000 warriors. But the Europeans had steel swords and lances, crossbows, guns, and horses – animals never seen before in America – while the Aztecs were only armed with swords and spears made from obsidian, a volcanic glass. The Spaniards were also eventually joined by up to 80,000 soldiers from native peoples who hated the Aztecs. Motecuhzoma was

Crimes and Punishments

Aztec society had very strict laws.

Crime	Punishment
Wearing cotton clothes if you were a commoner	death
Building a two-storey house if you were not royal	first time, the house was destroyed; second time, death
Taking a bribe if you were a judge	death
Getting drunk if you were a nobleman	death
Getting drunk if you were a commoner	having your head shaved

Tenochtitlán

The Aztecs built their great capital city, Tenochtitlán, in around 1325 on two islands in the middle of Lake Texcoco. It was divided into four parts. They were called Cuepopan (place where the flowers bloom), Moyotlan (place of the mosquitos), Atzacoalco (place of the herons), and Teopan (place of the gods). Teopan was the central area, where the temples were. When the Spaniards reached Tenochtitlán in 1520 it was finer than many European cities. Hernán Cortés, the Spanish conqueror, called it 'something I had never dreamed of'. He captured the city in 1521 and completely destroyed it. Mexico City, the modern capital of Mexico, is built on the spot where Tenochtitlán once was.

An Aztec illustration showing the founding of their great city of Tenochtitlán.

captured by the Spaniards and died while in captivity.

In 1521, after a bloody battle, the Spaniards captured Tenochtitlán. Motecuhzoma's successor, Cuauhtémoc, was tortured to make him tell the Spaniards where all the Aztec gold was hidden. The Aztec empire collapsed, and Cortés founded 'New Spain' in its place. The new Spanish rulers of Mexico made many of the native peoples into slaves and forced them to become Christians. Many others died from the diseases that the Spaniards brought with them from Europe.

Part of an Aztec calendar with comments in Spanish. The Aztecs had a cycle of 20 days, called 'counting the days'. Each day had its own special symbol.

15

The Incas

The Inca people lived in the valley of Cuzco, in the Andes Mountains, an area which is now in modern Peru. From the 15th to the 16th century they conquered neighbouring peoples and became a powerful empire.

Rise and Fall of the Inca Civilization

Under Pachacuti (ruled 1438–1471) the power of the Incas began to spread. By 1525 the Inca empire extended for over 3,500 kilometres (2,200 miles) along the coast, and about 320 kilometres (200 miles) inland. Their roads were excellent. It was the greatest civilization in Central and South America.

Atahualpa, last king of the Incas, had just taken control of the Inca empire after a civil war when in 1532 he was captured by Spanish soldiers, led by Francisco Pizarro. Although there were only 200 of them, the Spaniards had guns and cannon, and used them to kill thousands of Incas. The Spaniards demanded a huge ransom of gold and silver in exchange for Atahualpa's life. Atahualpa was sure that if they were given enough gold, they would go, just as, according to Inca belief, the gods were

The ruins of an Inca city uncovered on the mountain of Machu Picchu.

not need mortar. The city perched on a mountain ridge, and could be approached from only one direction. Two walls and a moat protected it. Inside the walls were the soldiers' quarters. There were stairways all over the city, as it was set on a slope. Raised channels, or aqueducts, carried water. There were temples, and a central square, the Great Plaza, where people had gathered for public meetings. Near the square was a great carved rock, the Sun Stone, or Intihuatana. It was the holiest part of the city. There were many temples, and amazing burial sites in caves, with nearly 200 skeletons inside them. Each skeleton was in a sitting position, and personal possessions were buried with them. The city also had houses for workers of all kinds, as well as storehouses for all public supplies.

Machu Picchu

In 1911, Hiram Bingham, an American archaeologist, wandered high into the Andes mountains to the north of Cuzco, the old capital city of the Incas, looking for Inca ruins. With a local guide, he climbed through a forest that clung to the mountainside, towards the peak of the mountain Machu Picchu. Suddenly, ancient walls appeared in front of them!

When the site was cleared, an extraordinary ruined city was revealed. Some of the buildings were made with stones so perfectly fitted together that they did

Machu Picchu can still be seen today. It is from examining this wonderful ruined city that people have learnt much about Inca society.

The Inca Empire at its greatest extent.

Machu Picchu
Cuzco
ANDES

Francisco Pizzaro (1475–1541), the Spanish conqueror of the Inca Empire.

kind when gifts were given to them. After taking the vast amounts of gold and silver the Inca paid them, the Spanish killed Atahualpa, and eventually took control of the whole empire.

Religion

Inca religion was based on the worship of the sun. It was like Christianity in two ways. One was that the Incas believed that if a person did something wrong, he or she must make up (or 'atone') for it. Like Christian priests, Inca priests (who could be male or female) would tell the wrongdoer exactly what to do. After the 'atonement' was done, the sin no longer existed. The other way that the Incas were like Christians was their belief in life after death, in which people who had been good would be happy, while evildoers would go to hell. The odd exception to this rule was that the upper class *all* went to heaven, however they had behaved during life.

The Hundred Years' War

The War Begins Again

The Hundred Years' War, as it came to be called, between England and France had begun in 1337 when the English king Edward III had claimed that he was the rightful king of France. Hostilities had stopped for a time after the capture of Calais in 1347, brought to a halt by the Black Death and exhaustion on both sides. In 1355 the war flared up again when Edward's eldest son, the Black Prince, led a raid across southern France from Bordeaux to Narbonne and back. In the summer of 1356 the Black Prince headed north from Bordeaux to join up with the Duke of Lancaster's forces. In a mighty battle at Poitiers the Prince defeated a superior French force and captured King John II of France.

In 1360 a treaty was signed which gave Edward III much of what he wanted. Many lands in France that had belonged to the kings

Joan of Arc (about 1412–1431)

Joan was a French peasant girl. She claimed to hear voices of saints telling her to free France from the English and help Charles the Dauphin (the son of the French king) to be crowned king. Somehow she convinced the Dauphin of her sincerity and was allowed to lead an army to save Orléans. She forced the English away from the city, then saw the Dauphin crowned King Charles VII of France at Rheims in 1429. She defeated the English several times but was finally captured and burnt at the stake in Rouen.

Longbow and Crossbow

The longbow used by the English was the most deadly weapon during the war. Although the crossbow was just as powerful, it did not have the rate of fire that a longbow had. An expert English archer could shoot at least twelve arrows in a minute, whereas a French crossbowman could only fire three in the same time. The French hated the longbow so much that if an English archer was captured his two fingers would be cut off. The V sign used today comes from the English longbowmen taunting their French enemies by showing them their two arrow fingers.

The longbow was used in the siege of Brest castle in 1373.

of England had been captured by the French. These lands were now returned to Edward, and the French paid 3 million gold crowns for the release of King John. In return Edward gave up his claim to the French throne.

French Successes

The French were determined to make it hard for England to hold on to their new land. French army leader Bertrand du Guesclin, a clever and able fighter, avoided large battles and used 'hit and run' (guerrilla warfare) tactics instead, which were very successful. England had troubles at home too. Edward, the Black Prince, died in 1376 and Edward III in 1377. The war was costly and led to a revolt by the English peasants in 1381. In 1396 Richard II of England and Charles VI of France made peace again and for 20 years all was quiet.

The Final Years

In 1413 Henry V of England (ruled 1413–1422) claimed, like Edward III had done, that he was the king of France. He took an army to France and won a great victory at Agincourt. In 1420 he was accepted as the heir to the French throne and he married Catherine, the French king's daughter. Then it all went wrong. In 1422 Henry V died and his baby son Henry VI became the new king. His advisers constantly argued. Things became worse when, out of nowhere, a French peasant girl, Joan of Arc, appeared.

Battle of Agincourt, 25 October 1415

Agincourt was the last great English victory in the Hundred Years' War. The English troops were led by Henry V. The French mounted knights were cut down by the English archers with their powerful longbows. Many English archers were suffering from dysentery (a disease of the bowels causing diarrhoea) and it is probable that many of them fought naked from the waist down! French dead and wounded numbered several thousand, while Henry's army lost only hundreds. Amongst them was the Duke of York who was found without a scratch on him. He was overweight and quite possibly died from a heart attack.

This illustration, from a manuscript by the French priest Jean Froissant, shows a scene at the Battle of Agincourt.

She inspired the French to save the besieged town of Orléans, and had Charles VII crowned King of France. Joan was eventually executed by the English, but she had brought new hope to France. The French slowly regained land, and after a period of peace they finally defeated the English at Castillion in 1453. The Hundred Years' War was over at last.

Russia

The Golden Horde

From about 1240 to 1480 southern Russia was ruled by the Mongols, a warlike people who had a vast Asian empire. The Mongols called their Russian kingdom the Khanate of the Golden Horde. During Mongol rule the country we call Russia did not exist. Instead there was a collection of states in eastern Europe ruled by princes and held together by a common language, religion, and tradition.

By the mid-14th century the Mongols' rule in Russia was weakening because they were fighting among themselves. Then in 1480 the grand prince of Moscow, Ivan III (ruled 1462–1505), led a rebellion that finally defeated the Mongols and ended their rule. Now that independence was

Ivan IV, known as Ivan the Terrible on account of his harsh rule.

achieved, Ivan wanted to become the sole ruler of the states to the north-west of Moscow. He set about conquering these neighbours, forcing their princes to recognize him as their ruler. By the time he died Ivan III had managed to unite most of these states under his rule. The states were joined together, and the country was called Muscovy.

Ivan the Terrible

Ivan III's grandson, Ivan IV, was known as Ivan the Terrible because of his cruel and violent rule. He became grand prince in 1533, and managed to weaken the power of the church and the *boyars*, Russian noblemen, whom Ivan hated. The *boyars* plotted against Ivan, but he brutally stopped their plotting through torture and

Peasant and Cossack Rebellion

The Cossacks were a people of southern Russia, famed for their horse-riding skills. They were a free people, and were sometimes employed as soldiers by the tsar. In the late 17th century the tsar Alexis wanted to take away many Cossack privileges. A rebellion was started in 1670 by a famous Cossack, named Stenka Razin. He was the leader of a band of about 7,000 outlaw Cossacks. Razin encouraged peasants, who hated their slave status, to join him in fighting the rich landowners. Razin's force soon swelled to 20,000 people. The tsar, fearing the uprising, sent an army to suppress the rebels. The tsar's highly trained army soon crushed the rebellion, because most of the rebels were not trained soldiers. The defeated Razin was taken to Moscow, where he was executed by being cut into four pieces in Red Square.

Stenka Razin rallies his troops on the banks of the Volga river.

execution. In 1547 he married Anastasia Romanov, one of the family, who would later become the rulers of Russia. In the same year Ivan took the title tsar (emperor) of all Russia. Ivan greatly expanded Russia's territory – to the Caspian Sea in the south, and over the Ural Mountains into Siberia in the east. He died in 1584.

Peter the Great

The tsar who turned Russia into a truly great nation was Peter Romanov, who became known as Peter the Great (ruled 1682–1725). He transformed Russia into a modern nation, and spent much of his reign at war with other nations. In one conflict he defeated the Swedish king, Charles XII, who was one of Europe's greatest generals. This victory let other countries in Europe know what a great nation Russia had become.

The cathedral of St Basil in Moscow, built during the reign of Ivan the Terrible.

Boris Gudonov (ruled 1598–1605)

When Ivan the Terrible died in 1584, his son Fyodor became tsar. Fyodor's poor mental state meant he could not rule Russia. Instead, his brother-in-law, Boris Gudonov (about 1551–1605), ruled Russia for him. When Fyodor died in 1598 Gudonov became tsar. During his seven-year reign, Gudonov ruled wisely, although he was the first tsar to force Russian peasants to become serfs, which means they became like slaves, being the property of rich landlords. Gudonov was also a very insecure ruler. He had a network of spies and was ruthless towards suspected enemies. When he died Russia soon fell into a period of chaos known as the 'Time of Troubles'.

The Orthodox Church

The Russians are Orthodox Christians. The Orthodox Church in the east gradually moved apart from the Catholic Church in the west. In 1054 a great split opened up between the two churches when the Orthodox patriarch and the Catholic pope excommunicated each other. Whereas Catholics see the pope as the head of the church by the will of God, Orthodox Christians would only accept him as 'first among equals' with no special powers. The Russian Orthodox Church began to develop independently when the Russian bishops refused to accept an attempt to reunite the Catholic and Orthodox churches in 1439. Never popular with the Orthodox Christians, the attempt failed completely when the Ottoman Turks captured Constantinople, the centre of the Orthodox Church, in 1453.

Spain

In the 15th century Spain was made up of several kingdoms. The Christian kingdoms of León, Castile, Navarre, and Aragon spread across northern and central Spain. In the south lay the kingdom of Granada, the last Spanish territory belonging to the Moors, a Muslim people from North Africa. The Moors had conquered Spain in about AD 700, but during a period of struggle known as the Reconquista ('reconquest'), the Christians slowly recaptured Spain.

The Catholic Monarchs

In 1469 the two largest Christian kingdoms, Castile and Aragon, were united through the marriage of King Ferdinand of Aragon and Queen Isabella of Castile. Their combined forces completed the Reconquista in 1492 when they captured Granada. Known as the 'Catholic Monarchs', Ferdinand and Isabella set up the Inquisition, a court that killed or imprisoned people who did not follow the Roman Catholic religion.

The New World

Another important event happened in 1492. The explorer Christopher Columbus, in the service of Ferdinand and Isabella, discovered a 'New World' – America. Over the next 50 years most of the West Indies, Mexico, and Central and South America were brought under Spanish rule. The wealth of gold and silver found there helped make Spain the most powerful country in Europe.

The Rise and Fall of Spain

In 1516 Spain came under the rule of the Habsburgs, who were also rulers of Austria, the Low Countries (modern Netherlands and Belgium), and the Holy Roman Empire, which covered much of Germany and central Europe. The new king, Charles V, thus ruled a vast, although scattered, European empire, as well as much of the New World. Charles gave up the throne in 1556, and divided his empire between his brother, who got Austria and the Holy Roman Empire, and his son, Philip II, who got everything else.

Ferdinand and Isabella brought Spain under a single rule in 1492.

Spain's Enemies

There were many threats to Spain at the height of its power. It had to fight off the Turkish Ottoman Empire, which sought to expand its territories further into Europe. Between the 1570s and 1648 the Netherlands, helped by the English, fought to free itself from Spanish rule and became an enemy of Spain. In the 16th century there were religious wars in France, where the Catholics were fighting the Protestants for the French crown. For decades Spain poured money and troops into France to support the Catholics. A very damaging Spanish defeat occurred in 1588, when King Philip II tried to conquer his great rival, England. He sent an Armada of ships to invade England and return it to the Roman Catholic religion. The Armada was devastated, and Spain's military might was severely damaged. Throughout the 17th century Spain was frequently at war with France, which began to take Spain's place as the leading power in Europe.

Spain was at the height of its power when Philip II came to the throne. He inherited an empire that included the Low Countries, the Philippines, most of Central and South America, and territory in Italy and Africa. In 1580 Spain invaded Portugal, adding the Portuguese trading empire to its possessions. Other European countries were alarmed at Spain's power.

At this time in Europe, after the Reformation, people were divided over religion, and

The inquisition was a medieval church court set up to seek out and punish those who spoke against the Catholic faith. It was particularly severe in Spain.

Catholics fought wars against Protestants. Spain was a Catholic country, and played a major part in these struggles. The very heavy costs of these wars, both in money and lives, caused Spain to lose a lot of its power. The kings who followed Philip II were poor rulers, and by the end of the 18th century, although it still held a large empire, Spain's position as the mightiest country in Europe had gone.

Philip II (ruled 1556–1598)

Philip II was a very religious and hard-working king, who believed that he should defend the Catholic Church from the rise of the Protestant religion. In 1554 he married Mary I, the Catholic queen of England, but they had no children and she died four years later. She was succeeded by the Protestant Elizabeth I, and England became Spain's enemy. During Philip's reign Spain entered its 'Golden Age' of literature and art. Philip was an elegant man who loved books and paintings. Some of Spain's greatest artistic works were produced during the Golden Age, and Spanish fashions influenced the rest of Europe.

Conquistadors

The leaders of the Spanish occupation of America were known as conquistadors (conquerors). Their purpose was to conquer lands for Spain. When they saw the vast amounts of gold and silver to be found in the New World, they set about overpowering the inhabitants, often treating them cruelly. The conquistador Hernán Cortés took Mexico in 1521, which led to the destruction of the Aztec empire. Francisco Pizarro led the conquest of Inca Peru in 1533. Other conquistadors claimed Honduras and Colombia.

Portugal

In the early Middle Ages the south of what is now Portugal was conquered by the Moors, a Muslim people from North Africa, who also took over most of Spain. In the 11th century the Christians began to retake territory from the Moors. The Christian kingdom of Portugal was set up in 1179, and had expanded to its present size by the end of the 13th century. By this time, Portugal had built a navy and developed its trade with other countries.

During the Middle Ages, Europeans paid large amounts of money for exotic spices, silks, and other treasures from India, China, and the other lands of Asia. These goods came to Europe by way of the Middle East and the Mediterranean. Portugal was a long way to the west of this trade route, but it was on the Atlantic Ocean, and not that far from Africa. In about 1420 Henry son of King John I, began to sponsor expeditions to

explore the coast of Africa and to find a sea route round the continent to the Far East, so that Portugal could profit from this valuable trade. It was Prince Henry, known as Henry the Navigator,

Henry, known as Henry the Navigator, funded many voyages of exploration along the west coast of Africa.

Goa, in India, was captured by the Portuguese in 1510. The Portuguese attempts to force the Indians to convert to Christianity were understandably unpopular.

The windows of the Christ Church at Tomar are in the Manueline style of art popular in Portugal at the beginning of the 16th century. Elaborate decorations of seashell, coral, and other sea shapes were used.

who started the great period of European exploration, although he never went on a voyage himself.

The Portuguese Empire

Henry sent ships to explore down the west coast of Africa, looking for a route to the Indian Ocean. His sailors discovered a number of islands in the Atlantic – the Azores, Madeira, and the Cape Verde Islands – and claimed them for Portugal. But it was not until 1488, long after Henry's death, that the Portuguese explorer Bartolomeu Dias sailed round the southern tip of Africa. In 1497 Vasco da Gama followed the route Dias had discovered and reached India in 1498.

The Portuguese soon set up trading posts along the coast of Africa and India. By the mid-16th century Portugal had a network of trading posts and fortresses on the route to China, Japan, and the East Indies (modern Indonesia), where the Moluccas, or 'Spice Islands', were located. For over 100 years Portugal dominated the trades in spices, silk, precious stones, and porcelain. Portuguese missionaries also travelled to the Far East to convert the inhabitants to Christianity.

While Portugal was expanding its empire in the Far East, it was also developing a colony in Brazil. A Portuguese explorer named Pedro Alvares Cabral discovered Brazil by accident in 1500, when he was blown off course on his way around Africa. Portugal established large plantations in Brazil and brought thousands of Africans to work as slaves there.

In 1580 Spain invaded Portugal. The occupation lasted for 60 years, at the end of which Portugal's empire had weakened. Portugal did not have enough ships or soldiers to defend their territories from the Dutch and the English, who took over as the major trading powers in the Far East.

Union of Spain and Portugal

When King Henry of Portugal died childless in 1580, the Portuguese throne became vacant. Immediately King Philip II of Spain invaded Portugal and claimed the throne for himself, becoming King Philip I of Portugal. Philip did not interfere with the Portuguese government, allowing the country to carry on as before. His successors, however, were not so generous and treated Portugal badly. The Portuguese resented Spanish rule, and in 1640 the Duke of Braganza (or Bragança) rallied an army and drove out the Spanish, making Portugal once again independent. The Duke of Braganza was crowned king, becoming John IV of Portugal.

The Mogul Empire

At the beginning of the 16th century India was made up of many small states, each with its own prince. Most of the people in these states were Hindus, although there were by this time many Muslims in northern India. Then in 1526 the Moguls, Muslim descendants of the Mongols, invaded the north of India. Their leader was Babur. With the exception of a brief period from 1540 to 1555 when they were driven out by the Afghans, the Moguls ruled much of India for nearly 200 years. Much of their magnificent art and architecture can still be seen today.

How the Moguls Lived

Mogul emperors and their families enjoyed being rich. Both men and women wore

The emperor Shah Jahan. The Taj Mahal can just be seen in the background.

Akbar, greatest of the Mogul rulers, leads his army across the Ganges river.

Akbar (1542–1605)

Akbar was the most successful Mogul ruler. He had already been to battle with his father when he became emperor in 1556 at the age of 13. He was a skilled soldier, and doubled the size of the empire by taking parts of Afghanistan, Baluchistan, Gujarat, and Bengal. Although Akbar was a Muslim, he allowed Hindus (who were most of his people) to practise their own religion, build temples, and celebrate festivals. He gave them jobs and even married a Hindu princess from Rajputana. This way he knew there would not be trouble between the religions. Akbar introduced a new style of architecture in the Red Fort at Agra and the new capital at Fatehpur Sikri.

The Taj Mahal, built by Shah Jahna, was meant to represent the throne of God in paradise.

jewellery and earrings made of gold and precious stones. They dressed in fine silks and cottons. They ate imported food off gold and silver plates, and when they travelled they took enormous silk tents with them that needed several people to put up. Mogul noblemen had three or four wives and each wife had several slaves. They had stables full of elephants, horses, camels, and mules and military equipment always ready for battle.

How did the Ordinary People Live?

Many of the people in India were farmers who lived near starvation level. They were at the mercy of droughts and floods, both of which could lead to food shortages. Their lives were made worse by the taxes taken by the emperors – sometimes as much as half of the value of their crops. Children were taken into slavery and people who could not pay were beaten and then sold as slaves.

The Taj Mahal

Some of the best Mogul architecture was created during the reign of Shah Jahan (ruled 1628–58). He ordered the building of the Taj Mahal at Agra in 1631 as a tomb for his beloved wife, Mumtaz-i-Mahal, who had died giving birth to her fourteenth child. It took 18 years to build and is made of marble inlaid with semi-precious stones. It is situated across the River Jumna from the Red Fort, a famous Mogul palace. Here Shah Jahan had a small mirror inset in the wall so that he could look at the tomb of his wife without anyone knowing. He is also buried there.

Mogul Emperors	
1526–1530 Babur	1556–1605 Akbar
1530–1540 and	1605–1627 Jahangir
1555–1556 Humayun	1627–1658 Shah Jahan
	1658–1707 Aurangzeb

The Beginning of the End

Shah Jahan's son Aurangzeb was the last great Mogul emperor. In his reign the empire reached its greatest size but also became difficult to govern. Aurangzeb was greedy and violent and did not allow Hinduism. He was unpopular with everyone. In 1663 the Hindu leader Shivaji attacked a Mogul outpost and managed to take control of a small independent state. The Moguls were beginning to lose their power.

The East India Company

European traders first arrived in India in the late 15th century. The Portuguese, Dutch, English, and French all set up trading posts in India, exchanging silver for silk, cotton, and other goods. As the Mogul empire declined, the British East India Company (based in Calcutta) became more and more powerful.

The Caribbean

The Arawaks and the Caribs

Five hundred years ago the islands of the Caribbean were populated by Amerindian people. The most important of these peoples were the Arawaks and the Caribs. The Arawaks came from the South American mainland. They travelled north through the islands and finally settled in the Bahamas and Hispaniola (now Haiti and the Dominican Republic) in around AD 1000. They were fishermen and farmers. They grew beans, peanuts, sweet potatoes, maize, tobacco, and peppers, and lived in simple houses made of palm leaves.

The Caribs came from Guyana in the 13th century and settled in the eastern Caribbean islands.

They were more warlike and raided other islands in their canoes. They conquered Arawak settlements, taking the women as their wives. Even in the early 20th century Carib communities were found in which all the men spoke Carib and all the women spoke Arawak.

Black slaves are made to plant sugarcane, watched by a supervisor with a whip.

What Happened to the Caribs and the Arawaks?

There were also many wars between the European settlers and the Amerindians. Caribs and Arawaks were massacred or taken into slavery, where they often died of overwork. Thousands also died because they had no resistance to the diseases brought by the Europeans. There were 250,000 Arawaks on Hispaniola when Columbus arrived in 1492, but by 1550 only 500 survived. When the British colonized St Christopher, they killed all the Caribs who were living there.

Today most of the people in the Caribbean are the descendants of the African slaves who were brought to work on the farms owned by the Europeans, and the Asians who were brought as labourers when slavery ended in the 19th century. The Caribs were very brave and many people nowadays like to say they had Carib ancestors. There is still a Carib community of around 2,500 on the island of Dominica, and there are Arawak people living in Guyana.

For the unfortunate slaves brought from Africa the Caribbean was far from being a peaceful place.

The pirate Edward Teach, known as Blackbeard, attacked many ships in the Caribbean.

The Arrival of the Europeans

The arrival of the Spanish in the Caribbean changed the lives of the Arawaks and Caribs completely.
In 1492 Christopher Columbus sailed west from Spain to the Caribbean. Columbus thought that the Bahamas were islands to the east of India. Later travellers understood that these were different islands and named them the West Indies. Columbus called the first island he came to San Salvador. He found gold in the Bahamas, Cuba, and Hispaniola, and went back to Spain to tell people about it.
The Spanish sent soldiers and traders to search for gold and set up colonies on the islands.

The European Wars

Other European countries found out about the riches of the Caribbean, but of course the Spanish did not want to share the wealth they were taking from the islands. They patrolled the seas in their galleons (warships), and any foreigner who was caught was brutally killed.

To begin with, the other Europeans were happy just stealing treasure from the Spanish. French pirates attacked Spanish ships on the seas and took their treasures home. The English adventurers Francis Drake, Edward Teach, and Henry Morgan became rich by taking goods from Spanish traders. In 1600 Spain was still the most powerful European country in the Caribbean. But in 1623 the English arrived and started their first successful colony on St Christopher (now St Kitts), and in 1629 the Dutch captured a whole Spanish treasure fleet, dealing a serious blow to the Spanish.

After that many wars were fought in the Caribbean and the islands changed hands many times. By the beginning of the 19th century the British had the biggest share of the islands.

29

America: The New World

Christopher Columbus

Christopher Columbus was an Italian seaman who had read about the adventures of Marco Polo and was eager to make voyages of discovery. Most educated people at this time realized the world was round, so Columbus thought he could reach Asia if he sailed far enough west. He asked different rulers to give him money, ships, and sailors for a trip to the East Indies, hoping to get gold and 'glory for God'. Finally in 1492, after six years of trying, Queen Isabella of Spain agreed to finance this plan.

Columbus's three small ships were called the *Niña,* the *Pinta,* and the *Santa Maria.* As the time at sea grew longer and longer, the crew became terrified of sailing so far away from Spain. Columbus showed them a faked log (journal) which said that they had travelled a shorter distance than they really had. No one had any idea how far away the Indies were, including Columbus himself. They were all very relieved to see the Bahamas islands, off the American coast. Columbus was sure they were nearly at Japan. The ships sailed for three more months, visiting Haiti and Cuba, and then went triumphantly home.

Columbus led more expeditions to these new lands in the Caribbean. On the second voyage there was a huge fleet of 17 ships full of people

who were greedy for gold, and priests to convert the natives. Columbus became governor of a large colony, which took native people as slaves to do farming work. Many of them died either of illnesses such as smallpox brought by the Europeans, or in battles with the colonists. During these voyages, Jamaica, Trinidad, the South American mainland, and the Gulf of Mexico were discovered. Columbus insisted until he died that he had reached Asia, although other people had their doubts. The Caribbean islands were called the West Indies because of his mistake.

Amerigo Vespucci (1454–1512)

Amerigo Vespucci was an Italian who went on four voyages to South America between 1497 and 1504. He realized that Asia was further away than Columbus had thought, and announced that he had found a 'new world'. In 1507 a German mapmaker decided to call this whole continent America after Amerigo.

Columbus arrives in the Bahamas, the first expedition to reach the Americas since Leif Ericsson.

French Explorers

Most French people came to North America not to settle, but to trade for furs – mink, racoon, bear, fox, and beaver skins – and bring the Christian gospel to native people. Jacques Cartier, an expert navigator, looked for gold mines but never found them. However, he discovered the St Lawrence River in 1535 and claimed land near it for France. A sailor and soldier called Samuel de Champlain founded Quebec, the first successful French settlement in Canada, in 1608. Robert Cavalier walked and canoed thousands of kilometres trying to travel down to the Gulf of Mexico. He learned many Indian dialects and managed to make friends with most of the tribes he met as he explored the Mississippi River. He laid claim to the new territory he named Louisiana after King Louis XIV of France in 1684.

A 16th-century map of the Americas. The figures around it are Columbus, Vespucci, Magellan, and Pisarro.

Henry VII funded the voyage of Giovanni Caboto (known as John Cabot) to Newfoundland.

Early Exploration in North America

Another explorer called Juan Ponce de León accompanied Columbus on his second voyage. He was hunting for a 'fountain of youth' that he heard was in what is now Florida. He did not find it, but the Spanish came back to Florida when they needed more slaves for their gold mines in the West Indies. In 1540 another Spanish soldier, Francisco Vázquez de Coronado, was the first to travel through the American Southwest reaching present day Kansas.

English Expeditions

The first English voyage to America sailed in 1497. An Italian called John Cabot (born Giovanni Caboto), working in the service of Henry VII of England, sailed to St John's Island, Newfoundland, Canada, with his three sons, and claimed it for England. Sir Walter Raleigh organized many voyages of exploration, hoping to find Eldorado, a legendary land of gold believed to be in South America. After trying to set up an English colony in Virginia, he brought tobacco and potatoes back to Britain in 1586.

North America: Life in the Colonies

For the first hundred years or so after Columbus's discovery of America, most European people were more interested in the treasures of the Indies than in the open spaces of North America. However, some English people decided to try to find a better life in a 'new England'. Because travelling overland was difficult in the new country, most of the new settlements were near the coast or rivers.

Jamestown

In 1606 a group of people hoping to find wealth and adventure set out for America in three ships of the Virginia Company of London. They arrived in Virginia in 1607 and called their new home Jamestown, after King James I. These new settlers were not prepared for the hard work and challenge of their new life. Some were lazy, and even chopped down buildings for firewood. After two years, most of the original settlers had died from hunger, disease, or Native American attacks.

John Smith became captain of the colony in 1608 and gave them a stern rule from the Bible: 'He that will not work, shall not eat'. The settlers learned to build stockades around the settlement, to plough the land, and to protect themselves against the Native American tribes.

Tobacco

Finally, they discovered a crop they could sell, tobacco, which was easy to grow in Virginia and could be traded for supplies that they needed from England.

An English settler called John Rolfe brought the first tobacco

seeds to Jamestown from South America in about 1612. The colonists brought in slaves to help grow the tobacco, and then they cured the tobacco leaves in smokehouses. Virginia tobacco became very popular in Britain, even though King James said it was a 'loathsome, stinking weed'.

Jamestown eventually became the first successful English colony, although it fell into decay in the early 18th century.

Native Americans

When Europeans first arrived in America, hundreds of different tribes of native people were already living there. Most had a simple, traditional lifestyle, using wood or stone tools. They did not have horses or wheeled vehicles. In the Great Plains, nomadic (travelling) tribes hunted buffalo, while Pueblo Indians in the southwest lived in villages. East coast tribes used wooden canoes for fishing or hunted and trapped animals. Some lived in wigwams, gathering fruit, nuts, roots, and herbs. Some were friendly with the settlers, but others battled with them over land. In the end, many Native Americans were driven off their land or died of diseases brought by the settlers.

Puritan families prepare to depart from Delft in Holland.

First Thanksgiving Day

The local tribe of Wampanoag Indians taught the early Pilgrims how to plant crops, grind corn (maize), and find good fishing. After the first harvest in 1621, the Pilgrims held a feast with them to thank God for their survival. This was the first Thanksgiving, which is still celebrated on the fourth Thursday of every November in North America.

The Plymouth Pilgrims

The Puritans were Christians who did not approve of ornaments, robes, and rituals in the Church of England. They did not think that the Reformation had gone far enough. They wore simple dark clothes and believed in hard work and prayer. King James I and his government made it difficult for Puritans to practise their beliefs in England. In 1620 some Puritans set sail from Plymouth in England for Virginia on a ship called the *Mayflower*. Because the Puritan passengers came for the sake of their Christian beliefs, they are often called 'Pilgrims' or the 'Pilgrim Fathers'. On the journey, they signed the Mayflower Compact, which set out rules for their new life. In November the *Mayflower* landed in Massachusetts, further north than Virginia, and the Pilgrims called their new home Plymouth.

Although they were far better prepared than the Jamestown colonists, over half of the settlers died of

Puritan families set out on the long journey to America.

cold, hunger, and scurvy during the freezing winter. More Puritan families joined them, however, and 'New England' quickly began to grow. By 1700, 250,000 English people had settled in North America.

Age of Exploration

Beginning in the 15th century, a number of explorers set out by ship from Europe to find the rich lands of the East. They discovered sea routes to places never reached before by Europeans, where they could start settlements, open up trading routes, and bring back valuable goods.

Countries financed expensive voyages in the hope that they could find valuable treasures such as gold, silver, jewels, ivory, and silk. But they especially wanted spices – pepper, cinnamon, nutmeg, cloves, and ginger. Spices were important in preserving foods, making them taste better, covering up any rotten flavour, and probably even killing germs. Many spices came from the distant 'Spice Islands', the Moluccas, in the East Indies (modern Indonesia). For centuries spices, and other valuable goods from the Far East, had been brought overland through Asia to the Middle East and the Mediterranean.

East and West

Countries such as Portugal, Spain, and England were too far from this trade route to benefit from it. So they determined to find new sea routes to the East. In Portugal, Prince Henry

A record of Portuguese ocean-going ships from the 16th century.

The Treaty of Tordesillas

In 1494 Spain and Portugal divided up the lands of the New World between them. The Pope gave Spain all the non-Christian lands discovered west of a line running down the Atlantic. Portugal was to have the lands to the east of this line. John II of Portugal negotiated a treaty with the Spanish, signed at Tordesillas, Spain, which said that the line should be moved farther west. This shift allowed Portugal to claim Brazil when Pedro Cabral discovered it in 1500.

A rare plate from the 17th century; the letters VOC are the initials of the Dutch East India Company.

(known as Henry the Navigator) sent many ships out on voyages of exploration down the west coast of Africa. The Portuguese continued these voyages after Henry's death, and in 1488 Bartolomeu Dias sailed round the southern tip of Africa into the Indian Ocean. Nine years later Vasco da Gama followed Dias's route and reached India.

Realizing that the earth is round, the Italian navigator Christopher Columbus believed he could reach Asia by sailing west. In 1492, with the support of Spain, he discovered the islands of the Caribbean, which he thought were the East Indies, and on a later voyage went on to find the mainland of South America. In 1497, supported by England, another Italian, John Cabot, reached North America. Although they had not reached Asia, they had found a 'New World'.

All these discoveries led to a shift in power and wealth in Europe over the next two centuries. The Mediterranean Sea became less important as a trade route, leading to the decline of such great trading cities as Venice. Instead, countries with an Atlantic coastline, such as the Netherlands, England, France, Spain, and Portugal, benefited from the new trade routes, and began to build up overseas empires that would bring them great wealth.

Prince Henry's School of Navigation

Prince Henry (1394–1460), son of King John I of Portugal, set up a school of navigation in 1416. He employed geographers, mapmakers, navigators, astronomers, and boat-builders to assist him in his research. Explorers and sailors were trained at the school before they were sent on voyages. Henry is also known as 'Henry the Navigator', although he himself never travelled further than North Africa.

Navigation

Being able to navigate (to find out where you are, so you can steer the ship in the direction you want to go) is essential to sailors. By the 15th century astronomers had worked out the positions of the sun, moon, planets, and stars more accurately. These were the main tools for navigation, together with the magnetic compass, which had come to Europe from China. Devices such as the quadrant and the astrolabe measured the height of the sun or a star, so the captain could work out the ship's latitude (the distance from the equator). The ship's navigator kept a record of the direction, or course, the ship was steered in and the distance it travelled on each course. The navigator used this information to work out the ship's position, called a dead reckoning position. Dead reckoning wasn't very accurate because it was difficult to be sure about the course and distances travelled. When Portuguese seamen began to explore the open ocean in the early 15th century, they soon found out how poor dead reckoning was for ocean navigation. To work out the ship's longitude (how far round the world it was) an accurate clock that could work at sea was needed, and this was not invented until the mid-18th century.

Great Explorers

Early explorers faced terrible hardships and unknown dangers on their voyages. So what made them go? Some were fascinated by the stories they had heard, and curious to find out the truth for themselves. Many hoped to grow rich from trading the luxury goods of the East. Others wanted the glory of taking possession of some new land, and having it named after them. Some were determined to bring Christianity to non-Christian countries. For many it was a mixture of reasons.

Zheng He

Zheng He (or Cheng Ho) was a Chinese admiral during the period of the Ming emperors. He commanded hundreds of ships and thousands of men. He made seven voyages between 1405 and 1433, during which he visited many places including Java (in modern-day Indonesia), Siam (modern-day Thailand), Arabia, Africa, and possibly Australia. He brought home many things that were strange to the Chinese such as rhinoceros horns and a giraffe.

The great explorer Ferdinand Magellan led three ships through a passage from the Atlantic to the Pacific Oceans in 1520. It was named the Strait of Magellan after him.

Ferdinand Magellan (about 1480–1521)

Spain had found much treasure in America, but not a way to the East. In 1519 a Portuguese explorer called Ferdinand Magellan offered to find a way to the Spice Islands (the Moluccas in Indonesia) by sailing west, as Christopher Columbus had done. He set off with 5 ships and 260 men. Magellan discovered a narrow channel between the southern tip of South America and the islands of Tierra del Fuego. This was later named the Strait of Magellan after him. This took him into a great ocean that appeared much calmer than the Atlantic had been. Because of this he called it the Pacific ('peaceful') Ocean.

Crossing the ocean took much longer than expected, and many of the sailors died of scurvy, a disease caused by a poor diet and not having enough vitamin C. Magellan was killed in the Philippines in 1521 and Juan Sebastian del Cano took over. Finally they reached the Spice Islands. The single remaining seaworthy ship sailed home with a cargo of spices. At the end of the three-year voyage, only one ship and 18 Europeans made it home. This was the first expedition to actually go all the way around the world.

Bartolomeu Dias

The Portuguese tried for over 50 years to get to the southern tip of Africa. In 1488 Bartolomeu Dias was exploring the west coast of Africa when a storm blew his ship south for 13 days. He realized that he must have come to the tip of Africa, but his frightened crew made him turn back. They thought they had come to the end of the world. Dias called his discovery the Cape of Storms, but the king of Portugal renamed it the Cape of Good Hope, hoping it was a route to the East.

Before the great voyages of exploration people had little idea of what most of the world looked like. This map dates from 1486.

Vasco da Gama

Dias helped another Portuguese explorer called Vasco da Gama to plan a voyage to India in 1497. After his four ships sailed around Africa, an Indian sailor showed them the way across the ocean to Calicut, in southern India. Although Africans, Indians, and Arabs had used this route for centuries, da Gama was the first European to reach India by sea.

→ Zheng He's seventh expedition
→ Bartolomeu Dias
→ Vasco da Gama's first voyage
→ Ferdinand Magellan and Juan Sebastian del Cano

Hard Life at Sea

Life was not easy for sailors. They were often cold and wet, and although pirate attacks and shipwrecks were a deadly danger, bad food caused even more problems. The sailors' main food, hardened bread called ship's biscuit, got infested with maggots, and the drinking water became green and stinking. Many sailors became ill with scurvy, from the lack of vitamin C in fresh fruit and vegetables. Those who died were thrown overboard to a watery grave. It was not unusual for half the crew to have died before the end of a long journey.

Arctic Explorers

To avoid the routes claimed by Portugal and Spain, northern Europeans had to find a different way to the East. The English tried to go northwest, to the north of Canada, but were stopped by huge icebergs. A Dutchman called Willem Barents looked for a northeast route in 1594, to the north of Russia. On his last voyage his ship was crushed by ice and the crew had to survive a freezing Arctic winter.

The Slave Trade

There has been slavery since ancient times. It existed in Europe, the Middle East, Asia, and the Americas. In the Middle Ages, Arab traders began to bring back slaves from the east coast of Africa, and sold them in the countries around the Mediterranean Sea and Indian Ocean.

People did not always remain slaves all their lives. For example, Malik Ambar, who became the ruler of Ahmadnagar in India from 1607 to 1626 was once sold as a slave to an Arab judge. In Africa itself, people were sometimes made slaves for a certain time to punish them for a crime or for owing money. They were usually treated well and allowed to marry or own property.

The Slave Trade in the Americas

The slave trade began to expand when the Spanish and Portuguese started to explore the Americas in the 15th century. In 1493, the year after he first arrived in the West Indies, Christopher Columbus brought sugar-cane plants to the islands. The Spanish tried to get the Native American peoples to work on their large sugar farms, called plantations. But many of them died from bad treatment and illness. So the Spanish brought African slaves to work on the plantations instead. In the 1540s the Portuguese set up sugar plantations in Brazil, and also began to import African slaves. By 1640 the Spanish and Portuguese had brought more than half a million Africans as slaves to Central and South America.

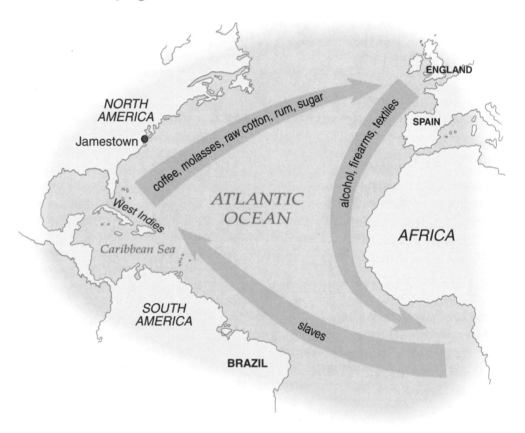

John Hawkins, English Slave Captain

John Hawkins (1532–1595) and his cousin Francis Drake began the English triangular trade. Hawkins sailed to Sierra Leone in West Africa in 1562 with goods to trade. He then bought slaves, chained them together, and took them in his ship to Hispaniola in the Caribbean. He sold them to the Spanish plantation owners and bought goods such as sugar to sell in Europe. When he returned, Hawkins advertised his new trade with a coat-of-arms showing a black man in chains.

In North America, the English set up their first colony in Jamestown, Virginia, in 1607. They set up tobacco plantations, but they did not like doing the backbreaking work themselves. In 1619 they began to bring over African workers to do it. After 1660 they brought over Africans as slaves.

Slaves were kept in cramped horrifying conditions on board ship, shakled in chains and anklets like the one shown here. Many died on the voyage across the Atlantic.

The Effects of Slavery

The European slave traders made lots of money. So did the plantation owners, because they did not pay the slaves. The slave trade made the European countries involved very wealthy indeed. Some African rulers, who were successful slave traders, did well too. But for most West Africans it was a disaster. The Europeans encouraged wars between African states so there would be more prisoners-of-war to sell as slaves. Many young, healthy people were taken away, and traditional ways of life broke down.

Life as a Slave

Life as a slave was extremely tough. Everyone had to work. Children, old people, and the sick did light work, such as weeding. Strong slaves, both men and women, did the hard jobs, such as cutting the sugar-cane. If they did not work hard enough, the slave drivers would whip them. The slaves worked from about five in the morning until six at night, with only two short breaks. Sunday was the only day off.

The Republic of Palmares

Many slaves fought their masters. Some African slaves in Brazil ran away and founded the Republic of Palmares in 1605. There were 10,000 people living there, ruled by an elected African chief called the Ganga Zumba (Great Lord). At the time, the Portuguese and the Dutch were fighting for control of Brazil. They tried to take over Palmares 20 times during the 17th century. In the end the Portuguese captured it in 1694.

The Renaissance: Rebirth of Thought

At the start of the 14th century some educated people in Europe had become fascinated by the ancient Greeks and Romans. These scholars began to search the libraries of monasteries for manuscripts that were many hundreds of years old. They longed for the elegant culture of classical times – poetry, literature, politics, and art – to be reborn in their own age.

This was the start of a movement called the Renaissance. The word Renaissance means 'rebirth'. It was a new way of looking at the world, and even a new way of thinking. Some people see it as the start of the Modern Age. The scholars of the Renaissance are known as humanists, because they were less interested in the doings of God, and more interested in the doings of human beings.

One of the first people to champion the study of the ways of the Romans was the Italian poet Petrarch. He founded a way of thinking that came to be called humanism. Humanists believed in having respect for individuals and that human values were just as important as religious ones.

The great Italian poet Petrarch. His work had a lasting influence on the development of poetry.

Petrarch was tired of medieval universities with their teaching about logic and church law. He was fascinated by the way things had been done in the ancient world. Petrarch passed his enthusiasm for the past to others. He wanted subjects such as ethics (morals), history, rhetoric (argument), poetry, and grammar to be taught just as they were in ancient Rome. The ideal person for the Renaissance humanists was the 'universal man': someone talented in all subjects.

An Age of Questioning

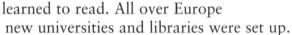

By the middle of the 16th century Renaissance ideas had spread from Italy all over Europe. This spread of ideas was helped enormously by the invention of printing in the mid-15th century. Many more books could now be produced, and many more ordinary people learned to read. All over Europe new universities and libraries were set up.

People were trying to make sense of the world through their own reading and thinking rather than just accepting what the Roman Catholic Church said. The willingness to question the authority of the church led to the Reformation, which saw Christianity split into Protestantism and Catholicism. It also led to the beginnings of modern science, with astronomers such as Copernicus and Galileo working out from their observations that the earth goes round the sun, and not the other way round as the church taught. This curiosity was sometimes dangerous because the church could severely punish people who disagreed with its teachings.

Erasmus (about 1466–1536)

Erasmus of Rotterdam was one of the most famous humanist scholars of the Renaissance. He loved philosophy, but was also religious. His writings made people laugh at ignorance and selfishness, and wrongs in the church, and he travelled 'wherever there were friends, books, and a printing press'.

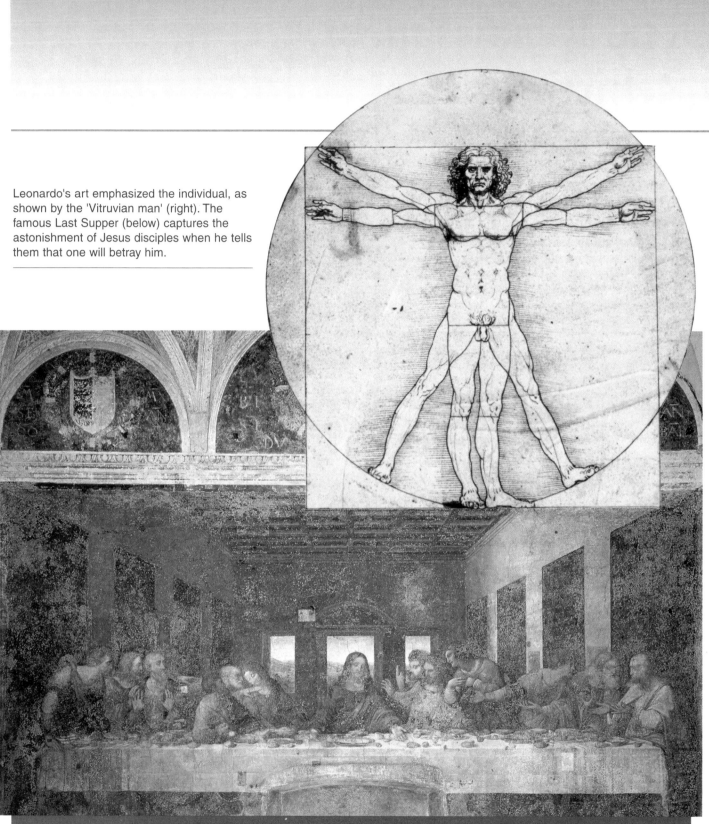

Leonardo's art emphasized the individual, as shown by the 'Vitruvian man' (right). The famous Last Supper (below) captures the astonishment of Jesus disciples when he tells them that one will betray him.

Leonardo, Universal Man (1452–1519)

Leonardo da Vinci was an Italian artist who also had a great many other talents. He is considered a genius, a true 'universal man' of the Renaissance. He was not only a great painter, but also an architect, engineer, inventor, and scientist. His many notebooks – written in mirror writing – showed his designs and interest in all kinds of science. He made accurate anatomical drawings and a model for a submarine.

Leonardo tried lots of experiments, leaving plenty of projects unfinished and making some bad mistakes along the way. One experiment with making a flying machine left his assistant with a broken leg! His famous painting of Jesus and the disciples, *The Last Supper,* began to crack because of the new type of paint that Leonardo had invented.

The Renaissance: Rebirth of Art

People of the Italian Renaissance felt that the Middle Ages were a time of imprisonment from which they were finally able to escape. They rejected everything Gothic – medieval art, architecture, and handwriting – and tried to copy the classical art of earlier times. For example, they used italic script because they thought (mistakenly) that it had been used by the ancient Romans.

St Augustine in his Cell, a painting by Sandro Botticelli, one of the greatest artists of the Renaissance.

Patrons

In 1400 Florence was a city-state, an independent city that controlled its own affairs. It was one of the richest cities in Europe. Very rich and powerful families became patrons of the arts. They were able to pay for important works of art or building projects and support writers, artists, and scientists.

The Medici family were among the great patrons of the Italian Renaissance. They were originally merchants and bankers but grew in importance. Cosimo de'Medici (1389–1464) ruled Florence from 1434 until his death. He patronized the arts, giving support to Fra Angelico, Donatello, and Lorenzo Ghiberti among others. Cosimo's grandson, Lorenzo the Magnificent (1449–1492), surrounded himself with poets, philosophers, and painters, including Sandro Botticelli, Leonardo da Vinci, and Michelangelo. Lorenzo used state money to recover losses made by Medici business interests, yet he was popular with his people and kept up Florence's place in Italian politics.

A Lifetime's Work

A huge amount of skill and a great deal of work went into the creation of a work of art. Lorenzo Ghiberti (about 1381–1455), is best known for his bronze doors for the Baptistery in Florence. Between 1403 and 1424, he worked on 28 bronze high reliefs for his first set of doors. In 1425, Ghiberti was commissioned to do the second pair of doors for the Baptistery. This consisted of ten pictorial reliefs, numerous figures and busts, and a decorated frame. The reliefs were cast by 1437 and installed by 1452. Ghiberti's bronzes are among the masterworks of the early Renaissance.

The Progress of Painting

Between 1417 and 1420 the Florentine architect Filippo Brunelleschi painted two panels demonstrating new schemes of perspective that set the style for all subsequent perspective painting in the Renaissance. He may have discovered these techniques in his architectural studies. Andrea Mantegna (1431–1506) carried out experiments in perspective in his painting that influenced almost every artist of the time in northern Italy. His first major project, the decoration of parts of the Ovetari Chapel in Padua, made use of perspective to make figures and buildings seem to recede up and away from the observer.

The Renaissance came to an end in the late 16th century as Italy came under foreign influence and the splitting of the Christian church in the Reformation and the Counter-Reformation brought new influences to bear on artists.

The ceiling of the Sistine Chapel in Rome, painted by Michelangelo, is one of the master works of world art. It has been said that Michelangelo was the greatest artist the Western world has ever produced.

Frescoes

One special kind of art of the Renaissance was fresco painting. The word fresco means 'fresh' because the artist painted his design onto a freshly plastered wall before it dried, which gave it a glowing colour. Frescoes were hard to paint because if the artist made a mistake, he had to chip off the surface and start again.

Northern Artists

Many other gifted artists flourished during the time of the Renaissance. In 1495 the painter Albrecht Dürer (1471–1528) went to Italy to study art. He was keen to bring the modern style to his native Germany, and made many beautiful woodcuts and engravings. Dürer's prints were inexpensive enough for ordinary people to buy. Hans Holbein (about 1497–1543) was another important German painter, and his speciality was realistic portraits. Pieter Bruegel (about 1525–1569), who painted landscapes and scenes of peasant life, is considered the greatest Flemish (Belgian) painter of the 16th century.

Michelangelo (1475–1564)

One of the greatest artists of the Renaissance, and of all time, was Michelangelo. His masterpiece, the fresco ceiling of the Sistine Chapel, is full of realistically painted people, and even God is painted as if he were a human being. Michelangelo was also a brilliant architect and even wrote poetry. But his greatest love was sculpture. He believed that locked in a piece of stone was a figure that needed only the sculptor's hammer and chisel to free it. His massive, powerful statues of people have straining muscles and bulging veins, showing how carefully he studied the human body.

Music and Theatre

Hundreds of years ago there was no recorded music, television, or cinema, so people had to make their own entertainment. Guests at parties might be expected to join in with the singing, or to play a piece of music. Kings were surrounded by court musicians who wrote songs for dances and plays and set poetry to music. Some of the popes were great patrons of music and employed many composers to create beautiful pieces for church ceremonies.

Well-to-do people would often hire musicians to entertain them.

Ancient Influences

People of the Renaissance admired the ancient Greeks and Romans, but they could only guess at how ancient music might have sounded from old writings. There was no music written down in notes from that time. Renaissance composers were inspired by the Greek philosopher Pythagoras, who said that musical scales should ascend or descend according to fixed mathematical intervals (spaces) of fifths (the pentatonic scale) and eighths (octaves).

Singing in Parts

Some kinds of part singing became popular at this time, such as rounds. 'Three Blind Mice' has been sung since the days of Queen Elizabeth I! Madrigals, unaccompanied songs where voices weave together parts of the melody, were first composed in Italy and became very popular in England.

Instruments

One of the most popular Renaissance instruments was the lute. It was a little like a

William Shakespeare (1564–1616)

One of the most famous playwrights of all time is William Shakespeare. He was born in Stratford-on-Avon, England, in 1564, and married Anne Hathaway at the age of 18. He joined England's leading theatre company, regularly performing for Queen Elizabeth I. In 1599 the famous Globe Theatre was built in London for the company.

Shakespeare wrote many plays, at least 38, some of which he also acted in himself. Some of his best-known plays are *Romeo and Juliet*, *A Midsummer Night's Dream*, *Henry V*, *Julius Caesar*, *Macbeth*, and *Hamlet*. The beauty and magic of his words, his imagination, and his amazing understanding of people's deepest feelings and secret thoughts still fascinate audiences and readers. He is often very funny, too!

Travelling companies of professional comedy players first appeared in Italy in the mid-16th century.

The Globe was the most famous theatre of Elizabethan London. A complete replica was built in 1995.

guitar, and the body was shaped like half a pear with a bent top. Violins, violas, and 'cellos appeared for the first time in the 16th century and started to take the place of an older family of stringed instruments called viols. Organs and harpsichords were popular keyboard instruments.

Around 1600 a new kind of musical style developed. It became known as Baroque, and was ornamental and complex in style. The first operas, an art form that combines acting, singing, and music, were performed at this time.

Reformation Music

When Protestants broke away from the Roman Catholic Church, they needed new songs for their worship. The German religious reformer Martin Luther began publishing books of hymns. He wrote some of the tunes himself; others were from old church music or folksongs, or even street songs. The French reformer John Calvin, however, who insisted that churches be bare and plain, allowed only Psalms from the Bible to be sung, without any instruments or harmonizing.

Theatre

In the Middle Ages mystery or miracle plays were performed for church festivals. Actors on wagons would act out scenes from Bible stories for everyone to watch. Then, when ancient books of Greek tragedies and comedies were discovered in Renaissance Italy, a new, more modern style of theatre began. Around 1550 women started to act on stage for the first time (although they did not do so in England until 1660). Before that men took women's roles. Some famous clowns also made their appearance: Harlequin, who is an acrobat famous for his multi-coloured costumes, and Pulcinella, who later turned into Punch in English Punch and Judy shows.

Inventions and Discoveries

Between 1351 and 1700 many important things were discovered or invented, things that made it possible for all the great advances in science that came later.

around 1450 German printer Johann Gutenberg perfected his printing press using movable type.

1504 Peter Henlein invented the watch in Germany.

1543 Polish astronomer Copernicus put forward the theory that the Earth moves around the Sun.

1576–1596 Danish astronomer Tycho Brahe made a catalogue of the stars.

1590 The first microscope was made in the Netherlands.

1608 Dutch optician Hans Lippershey made the first telescope.

1610 Italian astronomer Galileo discovered Jupiter's moons.

1614 Scottish mathematician John Napier published the first table of logarithms, which allowed difficult calculations to be made quickly and easily.

1637 French philosopher and mathematician René Descartes published his book *Geometry*, in which he showed how events in the physical world can be described mathematically and plotted on a graph.

Galileo (1564–1642)

An Italian professor called Galileo Galilei challenged many ideas of the ancient Greek philosopher Aristotle, which up until his time were still followed by doctors and scientists. Galileo established the modern scientific method, trying to establish general laws to explain observations and experiments.

By carefully watching a lamp swinging in a cathedral, he made discoveries about pendulums. He studied mathematics, and worked out that a cannonball fired from a cannon follows a special kind of curve called a parabola. He demonstrated that a heavy object does not fall faster than a lighter object, as Aristotle had believed. Galileo helped to improve the telescope. He spent many hours studying the stars and planets. Around

The trial of Galileo in Rome, 1633. He was arrested for supporting the idea that the Earth was not the centre of the Universe but moved round the Sun.

1612 he gave his support to Copernicus's idea that the Earth went round the Sun. In 1616 the church declared that Copernicus was wrong and warned Galileo not to defend the idea. In 1632 Galileo published a book that set out the arguments for and against Copernicus's view. He was summoned to Rome and put on trial for disobeying the order of 1616. He was sentenced to life imprisonment and confined to his home. Although suffering from ill health and eventual blindness Galileo, continued to work until his death.

1642 French mathematician Blaise Pascal invented the adding machine.

1643 Italian scientist Evangelista Torricelli invented a simple barometer.

1650 German engineer Otto von Guericke invented an air pump and English scientist Robert Hooke was the first person to see cells through a microscope.

1657 Dutch physicist Christiaan Huygens designed a pendulum clock.

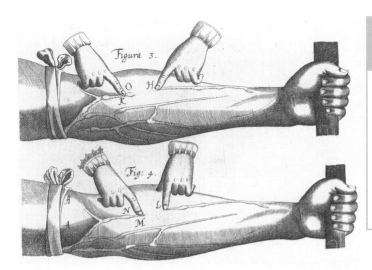

A drawing from a book by William Harvey showing an experiment to study the veins in the arm.

Discoveries that Healed

As people studied the world around them they began to understand more about the body and diseases. Several medical schools were founded, and in 1528, Paracelsus, a Swiss surgeon, wrote the first book explaining how to operate on people. An Italian surgeon called Gaspare Tagliacozzi did the first skin grafts. A Flemish doctor, Andreas Vesalius, found out more about anatomy (how the body is made) by dissecting human corpses, although at first people disapproved of using dead bodies for investigations.

In 1628 an English doctor called William Harvey was able to explain circulation – how blood moves through veins and arteries. Anton von Leeuwenhoek, a Dutch merchant, discovered single-cell protozoa, red bloods, and bacteria using microscopes he made himself. He realised that tiny blood vessels called capillaries linked veins and arteries.

1662 The Royal Society, formed in London to advance scientific knowledge, is granted a charter by Charles II.

1666 English physicist Isaac Newton discovered the principle of gravity and the laws of motion.

1680 The first clocks with minute hands appeared.

1698 English inventor Thomas Savery patented his steam-powered water pump.

about 1701 English farmer Jethro Tull invented the first farm machine, the seed drill.

Ambrose Paré, 'Father of Modern Surgery' (1510–1590)

A great French surgeon called Ambrose Paré invented false arms and legs for wounded soldiers in the 16th century. He also showed that to stop people from bleeding to death, it was better to tie off blood vessels than to burn them with a hot iron or boiling oil, which was the usual practice. He realized that wounds needed to be kept clean. He was a humble man and said about patients who got well, 'I treated them, God cured them'.

Isaac Newton demonstrates how white light can be split into a spectrum of colours.

Sir Isaac Newton (1643–1727)

Isaac Newton began to do experiments using a prism to split up a beam of light and proved that white light is made up of a spectrum of colours, like the colours of the rainbow. Newton went on studying the natural world, and from observing an apple fall down from a tree he formulated the theory of gravity – the invisible pull that draws things towards the centre of the Earth, and keeps the Earth and the other planets orbiting round the Sun. Queen Anne knighted him in 1705. Newton never stopped experimenting and learning and was an inspiration to scientists who followed him.

Sickness and Health

In the Middle Ages, and for a long time afterwards, people knew little about the human body and health. They did not know how important cleanliness was, and they did not have toilets or sewage systems to take away waste. Piles of rubbish, rotting animal carcasses, and dung lay in the street, and chamber pots full of waste would be emptied from upstairs windows even in the middle of the city. These unsanitary conditions led to the spread of germs that caused some deadly diseases, including the plague. Many people died young.

In Europe

Only rich people could afford the advice of doctors, but the doctors might do more harm than good anyway. An alternative was to go to an apothecary. An apothecary sold spices and drugs for treating illness, and could be called to visit sick

A 15th-century surgeon prepares to treat a patient with a head wound.

people. He might concoct his medicines from strange things like bat droppings or powdered earthworms! None of the drugs that we use today, such as painkillers, antibiotics, and injections to prevent disease, were available then.

Most people would use plants for medicines, making special herbal teas, moist pastes called poultices, or ointments from flowers,

Patients wait in a medieval convent hospital. Convents and monasteries were often the only source of treatment for the poor

leaves, or roots that were thought to heal diseases. Country people were experts at using herbs to treat illness. People guessed that a plant might show what part of the body it could cure by its shape or patterns. The walnut, for example, was thought to help to heal the brain. Some of these herbs really worked and are still used today.

If someone needed an operation, they might call a barber surgeon, who would not only cut hair, but also do operations like pulling teeth, setting broken bones, removing tumours, or even amputating limbs. There were no modern anaesthetics to use, so the patient might drink alcohol to dull the pain during the operation. Any kind of surgery was very dangerous for the patient because of the possibility of infection.

Around the World

Different kinds of health care, some more advanced than in Europe, were going on in different parts of the world. Arab doctors invented some medicines and surgical methods that were still used in Europe hundreds of years later. China had its own kinds of ancient herbal medicine and acupuncture, which involves inserting long needles into the body. Native American healers were skilled in the use of herbs and also tried magic for their cures.

People believed that illness could be caused by an imbalance of four liquids, called humours, in the body.

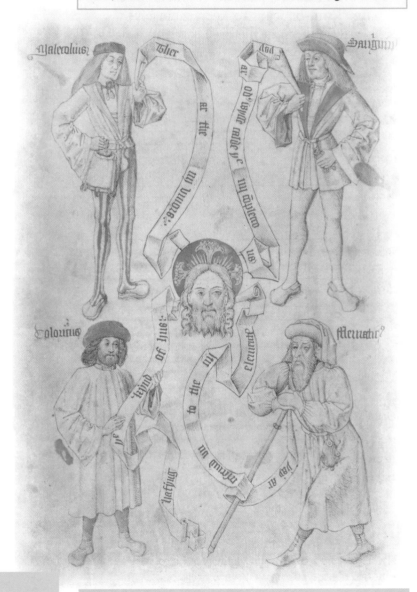

Plague and Fire

Epidemics

Dirty conditions in towns and lack of knowledge about medicine led to some huge outbreaks of diseases. These outbreaks, affecting large numbers of people, are called epidemics. Just before 1350 the Black Death, a terrible outbreak of bubonic plague, killed millions of people in Europe and Asia. Because people didn't understand the importance of keeping clean, or ways to keep themselves healthy, they thought of these epidemics as the result of bad air, or of God's punishment for people's sins.

Epidemics are more likely to happen when people live very close together in poor conditions, and during wars. During the English Civil War (1642–1649), many soldiers crowded into Oxford and there was an outbreak of plague there every summer. Infection was carried by people, or by rats on ships, from country to country. When the Spanish conquered Mexico, Central America, and Peru, the native people had no

A leather bucket and helmet used by people fighting the Great Fire of London in 1666.

resistance to European diseases like smallpox and measles, and millions of them died.

The Great Plague

Between 1664 and 1665 London suffered 'the Great Plague', the last great outbreak of bubonic plague in England. Bubonic plague causes huge, painful swellings called buboes on the neck, armpits, or groin. After a day or two, the victim would usually die. Many people

Fire Prevention

The Great Fire of London was probably one reason why the plague died out. It also made people think more about how to prevent fires. When London was rebuilt, some of the streets were widened, and brick or stone houses were built with tiled roofs instead of thatch. Better water and sewage systems were created and fire plugs were set into pipes, to let out water in case of fire. In 1676 a Dutch engineer invented a fire engine with leather hosepipes, and London insurance companies started fire brigades to protect their customers' property.

tried to escape from the city to the countryside, but often they brought the disease with them.

No one knew what to do to stop the plague. They tried burning strong-smelling herbs and washing their hands in rose-vinegar, or holding spices in their mouths to ward off the disease. If there were sick people in a house, it would be shut up for a month with a red cross marked on the door, and the clothes of the infected person would sometimes be burned. Different cures were tried, such as pressing a dried toad on the buboes! But thousands of people died anyway.

Daniel Defoe, the author of *Robinson Crusoe*, wrote about this time: 'It would have been present death to have gone into some houses. The very buriers of the dead, who were the hardenedest creatures in town, were sometimes beaten back and so terrified that they durst not go into houses where the whole families were swept away together'.

The Great Fire of London

The very next year after the Great Plague, in 1666, a huge fire broke out in London. It began in a baker's shop on a windy night and quickly spread through the city as the wooden houses went up in flames. A famous writer called John Evelyn wrote in his diary: 'All the sky was of fiery aspect like the top of a burning oven, and the light seen above forty miles round about for many nights'. The fire burned for days and was finally stopped by blowing up houses with gunpowder. Nearly half the city was destroyed. Beautiful buildings like the old St Paul's Cathedral, as well as ordinary houses, were burnt to the ground, and about 100,000 people were left homeless.

London wasn't the only city to have a terrible fire. Many other cities also had narrow, dirty streets with crowded wooden houses where a few sparks could quickly set alight neighbouring houses.

A dramatic painting of the Great Fire of London by an artist of the time.

51

Crime and Punishment

For centuries there was no police force in England, just local constables and watchmen to keep order. Townspeople were expected to look out for criminals and make arrests themselves. It was hard to enforce laws, although offenders who were caught often faced very harsh punishments. Perhaps because of this, juries did not like to convict accused people, even if they thought they were guilty, because they might be sentencing them to death. Before the law was reformed in the 19th century many crimes carried the death penalty. Crimes such as rioting, theft, and poaching were all punishable by death. Laws that were made favoured the ruling classes.

Highway robbery was a common crime, There was little chance of help on the lonely roads.

Moll Cutpurse (about 1584–1659)

Mary Frith, known as Moll Cutpurse, was a famous highway robber. She only attacked people who were enemies of King Charles I! A play about her life called *The Roaring Girl* was written while she was still alive. The word 'cutpurse' was used because people used to have their purses tied to their belts by cords. Thieves would cut the cords of the victim's purse and take their money.

Religious Crimes

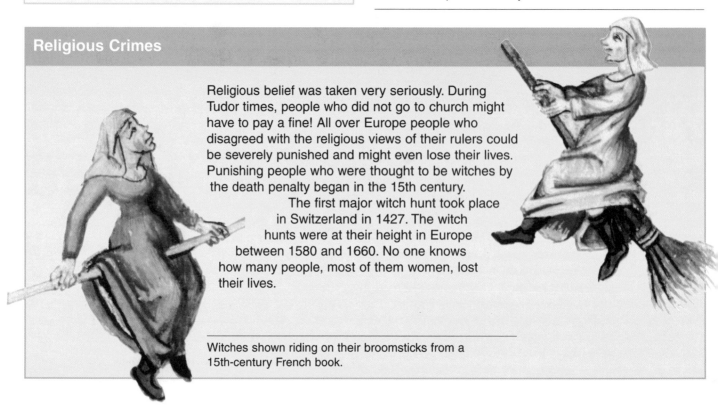

Religious belief was taken very seriously. During Tudor times, people who did not go to church might have to pay a fine! All over Europe people who disagreed with the religious views of their rulers could be severely punished and might even lose their lives. Punishing people who were thought to be witches by the death penalty began in the 15th century.

The first major witch hunt took place in Switzerland in 1427. The witch hunts were at their height in Europe between 1580 and 1660. No one knows how many people, most of them women, lost their lives.

Witches shown riding on their broomsticks from a 15th-century French book.

Bandits and Brigands

Plagues, famines, wars, and weak leaders all added to lawless times in Western Europe. Ex-soldiers often became homeless and turned to robbery when they were not being hired to fight. People who were running from the law, or who could not find work, might group together in gangs of bandits or brigands.

Towns had strong walls around them to protect townspeople against these mobs.

After 1650 highwaymen were a danger in Britain. They would hold up stage coaches, frightening people with flintlock guns. In France, highway robbers often pretended to be going on pilgrimage to fool their victims. Our word to saunter, to walk aimlessly, comes from the French *Sainte Terre*, the Holy Land. Vagrants seen wandering about might be greeted by the cry 'There goes a Holy Lander!', meaning someone who was pretending to be on a pilgrimage. The borders between Scotland and England were 'bandit country' for hundreds of years as cattle thieves known as reivers fought battles with each other and raided the local people.

The Duke of Clarence was accused of conspiring against his brother, Edward IV, and was put to death, rumour has it, by drowning in a vat of wine!

Painful Punishments

Sailors on board a Tudor warship could be tied to the mast and flogged on their bare backs with a cat-o'-nine-tails – a whip with knotted cords – for stealing. A sailor who killed another man might be tied to his victim's body and thrown overboard to drown.

Ordinary people were not often sent to prison, because it cost too much money. Execution or chopping off a hand or foot was quicker and cheaper. The thumbscrew, which squeezed a person's thumb, and other tortures such as piling stones on top of a person, were also used, often to get a confession. Tortures often ended in death, and were finally outlawed.

Humiliation of Offenders

Many punishments were carried out in public so that the person who had done wrong would feel ashamed. The ducking stool plunged people under water as a punishment for wrong deeds, such as fighting, swearing, and getting drunk. Other offenders would be locked in the pillory or stocks in the middle of a public square, and might even have to wear a fool's mask. People passing by could shout insults or throw rubbish to add to their embarrassment.

People often went to watch executions. Some felt sorry for the person suffering, but others found it entertaining. The gallows were often very high and the body was left hanging for some time as a warning to others. For the same reason, the heads of criminals were stuck on posts in public places.

The Reformation

A Corrupt Church

During the later Middle Ages some people began to think that the Roman Catholic Church had become corrupt (rotten). They resented the fact that greedy churchmen spent money extravagantly and led immoral lives themselves. Huge amounts of land were owned by churches and monasteries. The Pope seemed to have too much control, even over the rulers of countries. His words could not be challenged.

Indulgences

Medieval people were very frightened of the idea of being punished after death. The church taught that before they reached heaven, they would have to spend many years in a place called purgatory suffering for every sin they had ever committed. One way to get out of this was to

Martin Luther, who brought about the birth of the Protestant church in 1517 by speaking out against indulgences.

John Wycliffe (about 1330–1384)

John Wycliffe was a professor at Oxford University whose ideas were taken up later by Protestants. He believed that ordinary people should be able to read or listen to the Bible in their own language, and inspired the first translation of the Bible into English from Latin. The church considered this dangerous, because then common people would decide religious questions for themselves, instead of listening to the church, so it became illegal to read Wycliffe's Bible. His followers, called Lollards, were severely persecuted for their beliefs.

The first page of Wycliffe's Bible, the first time it was translated into English for all to read.

pay money to the church. Trading money for forgiveness was called buying indulgences. Much of this money from poor people's pockets went to fund grand building projects in Rome, where the Pope lived.

The Reformation was a movement that arose in the 16th century of people who wanted to rid the church of practices like indulgences and go back to ways that the reformers believed were more in keeping with the Bible, and particularly the New Testament.

Martin Luther

The Reformation began in 1517 when a monk called Martin Luther nailed a list of *95 Theses,* or opinions, to the door of the castle church in Wittenburg, Germany. These were a way of starting a debate about indulgences. Luther wanted to complain about the misuse of indulgences and other things he thought were wrong in the church. Thanks to the invention of the printing press, copies of Luther's arguments quickly spread around Europe and were discussed everywhere.

Four years later, in 1521, the Pope excommunicated Luther (threw him out of the church). Luther refused to take back what he had said if it could not be disproved by reference to the Bible. He went into hiding in Wartburg Castle where he started on his masterpiece, a translation of the Bible into German.

Luther wanted to reform the church and try to get rid of its faults. He believed that faith in Jesus Christ was required for forgiveness of sins by God alone, and that people could not buy their way into heaven through gifts to the church or good deeds. He also taught that people can listen and speak straight to God without a priest's help, and that the Bible is more important than church rules. Christians who agreed with Luther were called Protestants, because they protested against wrongs in the church. Many Roman Catholics wanted things to stay the same, however, and a big split in the church began.

The Reformation spread quickly through Europe. Countries such as Sweden and Denmark decided to become completely Protestant, but others, such as Spain and Italy, remained Catholic. Some people had Protestant beliefs even though their rulers opposed it, and faced severe persecution (they could be jailed or killed, or have their possessions taken away). In countries that became Protestant, the same thing might happen to Catholics. Throughout the 16th and 17th centuries there were battles and religious wars between the two sides. Meanwhile, Protestants split into different groups depending on what exactly they believed.

John Calvin (1509–1564)

John Calvin, a Frenchman, was another famous reformer. He agreed with some of Luther's ideas, but not others. He spent the last 20 years of his life bringing Protestant reforms to the often reluctant citizens of Geneva, Switzerland. His type of Protestantism, known as Calvinism, spread to many countries, including Scotland, where it was introduced by John Knox.

The Counter-Reformation

When the Protestants broke away from the Roman Catholic Church, the leaders of the church began to wake up to some of its problems. In 1534 Paul III became pope and started to reform the church from within. This was called the Counter-Reformation, because it was an attempt to counteract the effect of the Protestant reformers.

The Society of Jesus

In 1534 Spanish soldier called Ignatius Loyola began

The Council of Trent was an attempt by the Catholic Church to meet the challenge of the Protestant reformation.

a new movement for spreading the Catholic religion. This was the Society of Jesus, or the Jesuits. He was recovering from injuries received in a battle when he began to read about Jesus Christ and decided to devote his life to God. When he first became a monk, he lived in a cave and deprived himself of normal comforts. Loyola's army training showed in the way he stressed discipline and obedience in dangerous adventures. The Jesuits set up schools and colleges, and sent missionaries to Japan, India, and Brazil to spread the word about Jesus. The order of Jesuits is still active today.

Mystics and Musicians

Teresa of Avila was a Spanish nun who began to have trances and visions of God while living in a Carmelite convent. These mystical experiences were called ecstasies. She founded many new convents with the help of a monk called John of the Cross, who also wrote about spiritual life. Both Teresa of Avila and John of the Cross were made saints, and inspired many Christians.

The church paid for many new church buildings decorated with fine new paintings and sculptures, and commissioned much new music to make the masses grand and beautiful. All this helped to strengthen the Catholic Church.

The writings of St Teresa are still read and studied today by Catholic students.

The Council of Trent

Pope Paul III held three special meetings between 1545 and 1563 called the Council of Trent. Some important rules were made there, such as that priests, nuns, and monks should have to obey their promises to be poor. It was also decided that colleges for priests, called seminaries, should be started, so that church leaders would be better trained. They tried to think of other ways to spread Catholicism, such as sending out missionaries.

Persecution

Roman Catholic leaders decided to be tougher against anyone who disagreed with them or seemed to have false beliefs. The church ordered severe punishments for such people, who were called heretics. One of the worst examples of this persecution was in Paris, France, on St Bartholomew's Day 1572, when a massacre of the French Protestants, called Huguenots, began. In two days up to 20,000 Huguenots were killed.

Mary I attempted to re-establish the Catholic faith in England. Many Protestants suffered during her reign.

There was also persecution in England during the five-year reign (1553–1558) of Mary I. Her father, Henry VIII, had disagreed with the Roman Catholic pope, and he had made Protestantism the official religion in England. When Mary came to the throne in 1553, she brought back the Catholic religion. Many Protestants tried to escape to other countries, but around 300 were tried by the courts and then burnt to death because they would not become Roman Catholics. These deaths earned the queen the nickname 'Bloody Mary'.

Protestants also persecuted non-believers, people suspected of being witches, and Catholics. In England, during the reign of Elizabeth I (ruled 1558–1603), the Catholic religion was banned and a number of Catholics were put to death. In Italy in May 1527 an army led by Charles de Bourbon broke through the walls of Rome, murdering people, smashing up artwork, and stealing treasures. Many of the soldiers were said to be Lutherans and showed their disgust for the Pope. This violent event was called the Sack of Rome.

The Spanish Inquisition

One form of persecution was the Inquisition. It began in medieval times, but in 1478 a new Inquisition was set up in Spain by the Pope to check that people from other religious backgrounds like Jews and Muslims were following Catholic beliefs. Secret trials were held, using horrible tortures such as stretching the person on a rack. In the first ten years of the Spanish Inquisition, as many as 15,000 people were punished, and 2,000 were burnt at the stake.

More Developments in Religion

George Fox and the Quakers

The Englishman George Fox had very strong views about goodness and God. He asked people searching questions, demanding that they look at how they lived to see if their lives matched up to what Jesus had asked of them. Some thought him arrogant and judgemental. Others admired his uncompromising truthfulness.

Fox was a pacifist – he opposed all war. Yet he angered people so much because he was so difficult to argue with that they often attacked him violently. He ignored the rules of etiquette (how people should behave), which were based on class structure, and the belief that some people were superior to others.

A meeting of the Society of Friends, or Quakers as they became known.

Persian Shi'ism

Islam was founded by Muhammad in the 7th century. By 1350 it had spread across much of the Middle East, down through Africa along trade routes from the north coast, and likewise into India. Splits had occurred early on in the ways that different groups of Muslims practised their faith. The major groups were known as the Sunnis, who follow precisely Muhammad's original words, and the Shi'ites. The Shi'ites believe in an inner, mystical quality that can be experienced by the believer in contact with the imam (teacher). The Shi'ite movement suffered persecution, but it was adopted as the national religion in Persia (now Iran) in the 16th century and this strengthened the religion enormously.

A Muslim illustration from Safavid Persia. The Safavid Dynasty ruled between 1499 and 1736.

Fox believed 'we are all equal before God'. He was thought rude and disrespectful as a result. He lived through the English Civil War and the execution of Charles I in 1649. Oliver Cromwell's Protectorate followed, and then the Restoration of Charles II. Fox did not take sides in all this. All he wanted was for everybody to follow God's word.

Fox founded a group of people who wished to follow God in the way he taught. They were called the 'Society of Friends', and were nicknamed 'Quakers' because Fox said they should 'tremble at the word of the Lord'. The Friends were often persecuted for their nonviolent beliefs. Like other Protestant sects that opposed authority such as the Mennonites, many Quakers fled to North America. It was here in 1681 that another Englishman, William Penn, founded the colony of Pennsylvania as a refuge for Quakers. Quakers have had a powerful influence on American life.

Sikhism

In India around 1500 a man called Nanak founded a new religious community, in protest against the Hindu worship of many god forms. Islam inspired him to base his faith on one god who could not be represented by idols. Nanak taught that all people could reach God by meditating on the divine nature of creation. This faith was called Sikhism ('sikh' means 'disciple').

Nanak believed God had ordered him to preach this faith. He spent his life travelling and preaching, directing people to meditation rather than familiar rituals. He said people could be helped by a 'guru', a teacher or guide who is more aware of God, and who therefore can communicate God's nature and will to others. Nanak is regarded by Sikhs as the first guru. He was followed by nine more gurus. The last one died in 1708.

Persecution of Jews

Jews were constantly persecuted and chased out of country after country, even places they had lived in for many centuries. In 1492 many thousands of Jews were expelled from Spain, where they had lived for over a thousand years. They settled in Portugal, Italy, North Africa, and the Turkish Ottoman Empire, and some later went to the Netherlands and England. Other Spanish Jews chose to become Christian, so that they could stay in the land they knew and loved. Persecution also took place elsewhere in Europe. In Italy and Germany in 1555 Jews were forced to live apart in enclosed sectors of cities and towns, called ghettos.

Poland provided a place of refuge for many of the expelled and persecuted Jews, who settled there and prospered. By 1600 Eastern Europe was a thriving

The interior of a synagogue in Cordoba, Spain.

centre of Jewish life and learning. But in 1648 tragedy struck again. Ukrainian Cossack farmers rebelled against Polish rule. They identified the Jewish people with the Poles they hated, and massacred many Jews.

Books and Printing

Books for All?

In the Middle Ages books were a great luxury. Each book had to be hand-copied by monks in monasteries. Beautiful pictures were added to decorate the pages. Often books were written on vellum (calfskin) or parchment (fine sheepskin or goatskin). Because it took a great deal of time and work to copy them out, they were very expensive – only rich people and churches could afford them. There was no way of mass-producing books in Europe before this time, because Europeans didn't know about printing. In fact, hundreds of years before, Chinese people had invented paper, and how to print using images cut into wooden blocks.

In the 11th century they discovered how to print using movable type made of clay and wood. However, the complex characters of written Chinese were too difficult to produce as type.

In the 14th century Europeans discovered how to print with wooden blocks. However, the books made with this block method were still rare and expensive. A whole page of type had to be cut or engraved into a block of wood or metal, which could only be used for the one page.

Gutenberg's New Invention

Around 1450 a German goldsmith called Johann (or Johannes) Gutenberg began to develop a way of printing using movable type. The big advantage he had over the Chinese was the simple alphabet used in Europe. This made it relatively easy to produce all the letters that were needed. In this method, each letter was cut out of metal on a small, individual block. These blocks were put together on a printing plate to make one page of a book. After printing the page, the type could be rearranged and used again for the next page. Gutenberg's press was soon copied in other European countries, so many more books could be printed, on all sorts of subjects. Some people were suspicious of this new art of printing and even feared that it might be from the devil. It was hard for them to understand how books could be produced so quickly, or why all the copies looked exactly alike. But by 1500 there were as many as 1,700 printing shops in Europe, and several million books had been produced.

The invention of printing and the flood of new books changed language, as a common version was used instead of local dialects. This helped

The First Printing Press

Gutenberg created his first printing press out of a wooden machine used to press grapes or cheeses. He moulded pieces of raised metal type out of a mixture of lead and other metals, each showing a different letter or punctuation mark, and then arranged them on a tray called a form. After covering the type with a thin layer of sticky ink, he placed the paper on top. By turning a huge wood screw on the press, he would push a heavy wood block evenly against the paper. With his new press, Gutenberg could produce about 300 printed sheets a day.

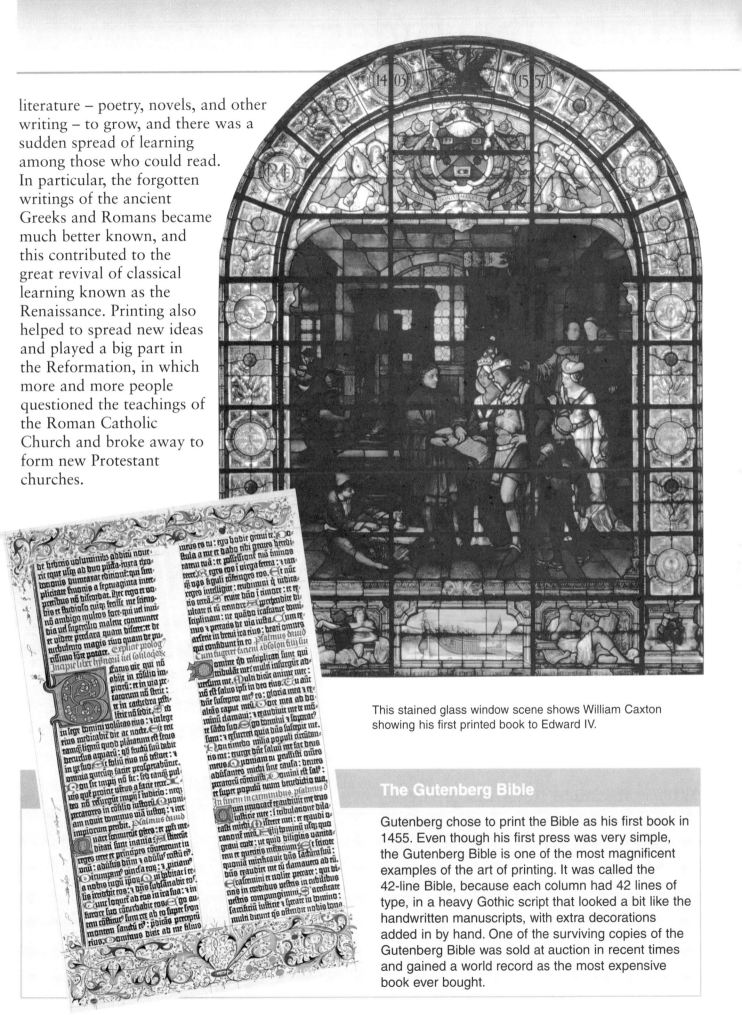

literature – poetry, novels, and other writing – to grow, and there was a sudden spread of learning among those who could read. In particular, the forgotten writings of the ancient Greeks and Romans became much better known, and this contributed to the great revival of classical learning known as the Renaissance. Printing also helped to spread new ideas and played a big part in the Reformation, in which more and more people questioned the teachings of the Roman Catholic Church and broke away to form new Protestant churches.

This stained glass window scene shows William Caxton showing his first printed book to Edward IV.

The Gutenberg Bible

Gutenberg chose to print the Bible as his first book in 1455. Even though his first press was very simple, the Gutenberg Bible is one of the most magnificent examples of the art of printing. It was called the 42-line Bible, because each column had 42 lines of type, in a heavy Gothic script that looked a bit like the handwritten manuscripts, with extra decorations added in by hand. One of the surviving copies of the Gutenberg Bible was sold at auction in recent times and gained a world record as the most expensive book ever bought.

Rise of the Tudors

Wars of the Roses

In 1485 Henry Tudor, Earl of Richmond, stood in Bosworth field. He had won a battle that ended the struggle that had unsettled England and its kings for the past 30 years. This struggle is now known as the Wars of the Roses.

The struggle started when King Henry VI (ruled 1422–1461 and 1470–1471) went mad in 1453. His cousin, Richard, Duke of York, took over as protector of the realm in 1454, but then the following year Henry recovered and wanted to be king again. He forced Richard to fight against him to keep the throne. The two sides fought off and on for 30 years. By the time the struggle ended, four kings had been crowned and had ruled England.

Battles of the Wars of the Roses.

Hexham
Towton
Wakefield
Blore Heath
Bosworth
Ludford
Northampton
Mortimers Cross
Edgcote
Tewkesbury
St Albans
Barnet

Sea Exploration

This was the age of sea exploration. In 1497, during Henry VII's reign, John and Sebastian Cabot sailed west, looking for China, and found North America without realizing it. During the reign of Queen Elizabeth, Walter Raleigh sailed to South America, seeking Eldorado, a fabled land of gold. Francis Drake sailed round the world in a ship called the *Pelican*. This ship was renamed the *Golden Hind* halfway round.

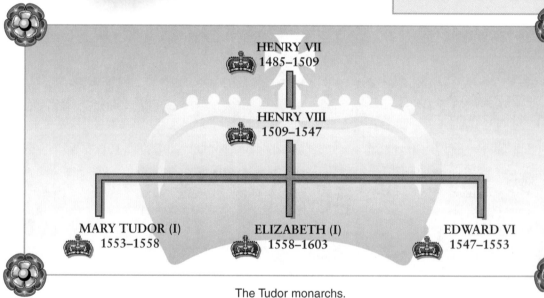

HENRY VII
1485–1509

HENRY VIII
1509–1547

MARY TUDOR (I)
1553–1558

ELIZABETH (I)
1558–1603

EDWARD VI
1547–1553

The Tudor monarchs.

Why is it Called the Wars of the Roses?

Two families, both descendants of King Edward III, wanted control of the throne. Henry VI's family was called the house of Lancaster, and Richard's family was called the house of York. The house of Lancaster had a badge with a red rose, and the house of York had a badge with a white rose. The name Wars of the Roses was first used by the writer Walter Scott over 300 years after the conflict ended.

Battle of Bosworth

In 1485 Henry, Earl of Richmond, landed in his native Wales from France to help fight against the Yorkist king Richard III (ruled 1483–1485). He killed Richard at a battle close to the village of Market Bosworth, near Leicester. He then became the new king as Henry VII (ruled 1485–1509), the first Tudor monarch. He was from the house of Lancaster, and ended the Wars of the Roses in a clever way. To make sure of peace, he married Elizabeth from the house of York, uniting the warring families at last.

Reign of the Tudors

The royal house of Tudor was to rule England for the next 120 years. Its symbol, the Tudor rose, was made up of the red rose of Lancaster and the white rose of York combined. Henry VII's son, Henry VIII, is famous for having six wives. He was very anxious to have one or more sons, to avoid any arguments about who should be king after him. Such arguments might lead to another long period of wars like the Wars of the Roses. Up to then, no woman had been crowned queen, so daughters did not count.

Henry could never have known that his only son would die after a few months as king, and that both his daughters would reign. Mary I was the first queen in English history to be crowned in her own right, and her sister Elizabeth I became renowned as one of the greatest English monarchs. Nowadays, when people think of the Tudor period, it is probably Queen Elizabeth I that they think of first.

The Tudor monarchs were strong rulers. Under their rule England became wealthier and more powerful. The arts flourished, explorers discovered new lands, and a new state church, the Church of England, was founded with the monarch at its head.

King Richard III at the Battle of Bosworth where he lost his crown and his life.

A portrait of Henry VII, the first of the Tudor rulers of England.

Henry VIII

A portrait of Henry VIII by the famous artist Hans Holbein.

End of the Monasteries

In 1529 Henry fell out with Pope Clement VII, head of the Roman Catholic Church, over Clement's refusal to grant Henry the divorce he demanded. As a result, in 1530 Henry called himself the only head of the English church, and in 1534 laws were passed making this final and official. Henry still regarded himself as Catholic, but other Catholics could not accept this behaviour. To silence his opposition and raise money, Henry began in 1536 to close down the monasteries. He took their land and their wealth, and sold it for his own purposes. A few cathedrals were built with the profits, but Henry used most of the money for his own expensive tastes.

When Henry VIII (ruled 1509–1547) came to the throne, aged 17, the people of England were delighted. He was tall, strong, handsome, generous, energetic, and charming. Henry's wife, the Spanish princess Catherine of Aragon, had been married to his brother Arthur, who had died at 15. Marrying a brother's widow was not allowed, but Henry had special permission from the Pope, head of the Roman Catholic Church.

Henry was used to being admired by everyone and having his own way. He and Catherine had a daughter, Mary. He wanted a son, or better, many sons. No queen had ever ruled England. If he died without a son his line would not continue and England might well be thrown into turmoil, with different groups fighting for the crown. Worse, a foreign prince might come and marry his daughter, and add England to the possessions of his country.

The Six Wives

After 20 years Henry decided he must get another wife. He asked the Pope to annul (cancel) his marriage to Catherine, because of her previous marriage to Arthur. The Pope refused, and Henry grew angry and determined to have his own way. He succeeded by taking England out of the Roman Catholic Church. This meant that the Pope no longer had authority in England and Henry became head of the English church. Henry ordered the execution of any of his ministers who disagreed with him. He then married Anne Boleyn, and they had a daughter, Elizabeth. Anne was accused of adultery (having a love affair with someone else) and executed three years after marrying Henry. He then married Jane Seymour. Jane died giving birth to their son Edward.

The unhappy Henry next married a German princess, Anne of Cleves, after only seeing a portrait of her. However, he hated the sight of her in person, and although he went through with the marriage, he managed to divorce her too. His next wife, Catherine Howard, was soon beheaded for adultery. Catharine Parr was his sixth wife. He grew irritated with her, but died before he had time to do anything about it.

A portrait of a young woman who may be Catherine of Aragon, Henry's first wife.

A view of Hampton Court Place, built by Cardinal Wolsey and later claimed by Henry.

Cardinal Wolsey (about 1475–1530)

The priest Thomas Wolsey was a clever young man who became an adviser to Henry VII. Young Henry VIII admired and trusted him. In 1515 the Pope made him a cardinal (the next rank in the church to the pope) and then Henry made him Lord Chancellor – his chief minister. Wolsey was a brilliant politician, and in 1518 successfully made peace with France after years of war.

Wolsey's pride and greed, however, made him unpopular. He built the grand palace of Hampton Court for himself, and closed down 30 monasteries and convents, using their wealth to build colleges. In 1529, when King Henry turned against the Pope for not letting him divorce Catherine of Aragon, Henry took away Wolsey's power and many of his palaces. In 1530 Wolsey was arrested for high treason, perhaps partly because Henry, who had become bitter and greedy, wanted his wealth. Wolsey died before he could be tried.

Elizabeth I

King Henry VIII of England had six wives, mainly because he was desperate to have at least one son to be king after him. One of Henry's children was to become one of the greatest monarchs in English history, but it was not his son, Edward. It was Elizabeth, Henry's second daughter. Her mother was Anne Boleyn, who was beheaded when Elizabeth was only three years old.

Elizabeth (ruled 1558–1603) was a bright child who wrote lively letters in Latin and Greek as well as English to her stepmother, Catherine Parr. She became queen in 1558, after the death of her Catholic sister, Queen Mary (known as 'Bloody Mary' because she had executed so many Protestants). Elizabeth restored Protestantism to England and brought peace and prosperity. She reigned for 45 years, longer than any monarch before. Her reign, however, was not easy.

A carved oak chair from the time of Elizabeth I.

People celebrate a wedding. Wealthy people lived well under Elizabeth.

A Golden Age?

The Elizabethan period has often been called a golden age. It was an age of great dramatists such as William Shakespeare, Christopher Marlowe, and Ben Jonson, and people from all levels of society came to see their plays. One of the most famous poets during the period was Sir Edmund Spenser, who wrote a long poem called *The Faerie Queene* in honour of Queen Elizabeth. Elizabethan England also produced many fine composers such as Thomas Tallis and William Byrd. For the nobility and other wealthy people it was indeed a golden age, and men as well as women dressed in rich, colourful clothes covered in jewels. But for the common people life was much as it had been for centuries. In fact, in some ways life became worse during the Elizabethan period, with higher food prices and unemployment.

Elizabeth and Mary, Queen of Scots

For years, Elizabeth's cousin Mary, Queen of Scots caused trouble. Mary was a Catholic, and the granddaughter of Henry VIII's older sister Margaret. Many people were still loyal Catholics and because of this Mary seemed to think she should, or could, be queen of England as well as of Scotland. Elizabeth did not want to hurt her cousin Mary – perhaps she felt there had already been too much bloodshed in her family. But Mary constantly seemed to be plotting, or to be the focus of plots, against Elizabeth and finally, reluctantly, Elizabeth ordered her execution. After Mary's death in 1587, Elizabeth angrily said she had not really meant it to happen.

A portrait of Elizabeth I painted to celebrate England's defeat of the Spanish Armada.

The Spanish Armada

Soon after, the Catholic king of Spain, Philip II, who had been the husband of Queen Mary, became angry with Elizabeth for her unfairness to Catholics and for the execution of Mary, Queen of Scots. He had once nearly been king of England as well as of Spain, and he still hoped for such a prize. In 1588 he sent a great fleet of Spanish warships, called the Armada, to invade England. Elizabeth inspired the English troops and sailors with a rousing speech, and, under the command of Sir Francis Drake, the English fleet swiftly defeated the Spanish before they could land.

The Virgin Queen

Elizabeth never married and was known as 'the Virgin Queen'. Although she wanted love, she knew that if she had a husband she would have to lose some, if not all, of her control over England's affairs. When she died aged almost 70, the crown passed to the only son of Mary, Queen of Scots. This was James VI of Scotland, who was a great-great-grandson of Henry VII, and who now became James I of England.

Religious Disagreements

Henry VIII had wanted to keep England Catholic, but with the king, not the pope, as the head of the church. However, under Henry's son, Edward VI, the country became truly Protestant. Many individuals remained Catholic, though. When Mary I came to the throne Catholicism was restored as England's chief religion. Mary was harsh towards Protestants, and burned hundreds of people who would not give up their Protestant faith.

Elizabeth again restored Protestantism, but, wiser and kinder than her father and her sister, she tolerated Catholics for many years. In her later years, however, as the Pope and the Catholic monarchs of Europe plotted against her, she took a harsher line, and many Catholic missionaries were executed as traitors.

The Spanish Armada

In the mid-16th century Spain was ruled by King Philip II, a devout Catholic. The Spanish empire was extensive, and Philip controlled large areas of Europe. Spain's conquistadors (conquerors) had taken over most of Central and South America, and were bringing back huge amounts of gold and silver. But Philip was using up these riches to fight wars against Protestants in the Netherlands who did not want to be ruled by Spain. He ended up in debt, and Spanish industry went downhill.

England, ruled by Elizabeth I, was now a Protestant country. In 1584 Queen Elizabeth sent 7,000 soldiers to help the Dutch rebels fight the Spaniards. This meant war!

Philip's Plan

Philip decided to invade England and score a victory for the Catholic Church. In May 1588 a great fleet called the Armada (the Spanish word for 'fleet of ships') was assembled. The ships had crosses marked on the sails to show it was a holy war. Before the Armada sailed, Philip tried to scare the English by telling them exactly what they were up against. There were 130 ships, nearly 19,000 soldiers, 8,000 sailors, and many guns, gunpowder, and cannon.

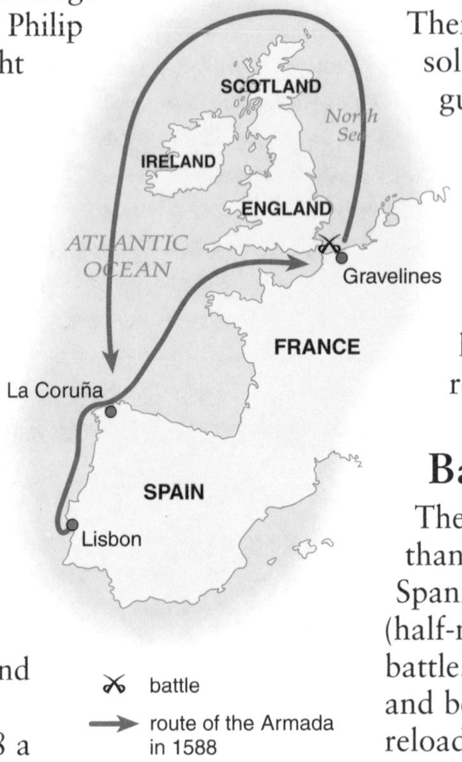

England got ready by planning to light fires as beacons on the hilltops and ring bells all around the country if the Armada was seen. This would be the sign for local people to get their weapons ready for fighting the Spanish.

Battle Tactics

The Armada seemed more powerful than the smaller English fleet. The Spanish put their ships into a crescent (half-moon) formation in readiness for battle. But the English had faster ships and better gunners, who could fire and reload quickly. The Spanish planned to

Francis Drake (about 1540–1596)

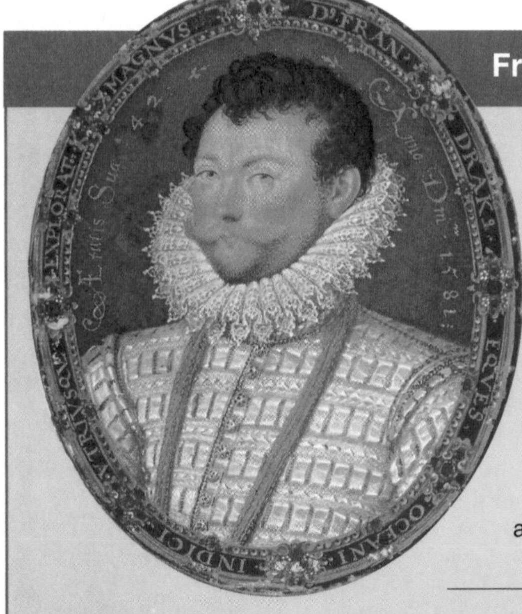

A portrait of Sir Francis Drake by the famous Elizabethan artist Nicholas Hilliard.

Francis Drake was an English slave trader. In 1568 he was nearly killed by the Spaniards in America, and from then on he attacked their ships whenever he had the chance, taking the gold and silver they carried from America. He became a famous privateer (a kind of pirate operating with the permission of his government), and was so successful at discovering Spanish ships that they thought he used magic!

In 1577 Drake led a fleet of five ships to explore the Pacific. Reaching the Strait of Magellan in 1578, he renamed his ship the *Pelican*, calling it the *Golden Hind*. Sailing into the Pacific, Drake went north, carrying out raids against the Spanish. He eventually set out across the Pacific, returning to England by way of the Indian Ocean in 1580. The *Golden Hind* was the only one of the five ships to make the journey. Drake was knighted on the deck of his ship by Queen Elizabeth.

When Elizabeth suspected that Spain was planning to attack England in 1587, she told Drake to strike the first blow. Drake daringly attacked some of the Spanish ships sitting in their own port, Cádiz. He bragged that he had singed (burned) the king of Spain's beard. This made him a hero in England.

A painting of the Spanish fleet by the 18th-century artist John Pine. The English fleet can be seen approaching from the right.

use grappling hooks to pull the English ships closer, and then send soldiers aboard to attack the crews, but they never got close enough to do this. At first, although lots of powder and shots were fired, few ships were sunk. This was because none of the guns could hit a target that was very far away. Then at night the English sent eight burning fireships (ships set on fire purposely) to drift towards the Armada, which made the Spanish scatter, sending them into disarray.

Victory for England

The biggest battle was fought the following morning off Gravelines, near Calais on the French coast. Each side shot holes in each other's ships, but the Spanish came out of the battle the worst off. They were out of ammunition and in danger of being driven onto the sandbanks near Calais. A sudden change in the direction of the wind carried them into the North Sea. A terrible journey around Scotland and Ireland lay ahead. The weather was cold and stormy, and many of the sailors died of disease or lack of food and water. Many of the Spanish ships were shipwrecked. In all, only 86 ships and half the men of the Armada made it back to the safety of Spain, some five months after they had set out with dreams of conquering England.

Suffering of the Sailors

Even when the last ships struggled home, the sailors' suffering did not end. Both English and Spanish sailors were starving, out of water, and dressed in rags. They had not been paid, and months later were still dying of diseases. About two-thirds of the Spanish soldiers died.

Elizabeth led celebrations in England, yet despite the terrible cost in money and lives, the war was not over. The countries kept fighting until 1604, when both Philip and Elizabeth were dead.

Civil War in England

Why did the War Begin?

The English Civil War lasted from 1642 to 1649. It was fought by the supporters of King Charles I (ruled 1625–1649) on one side and the supporters of Parliament on the other. The war started because of disagreements over religion, money, and who was to rule the country – the king or Parliament. The king's supporters were called the Royalists, or Cavaliers. Those on Parliament's side were the Parliamentarians, or Roundheads (because of the helmets they wore).

The king was the head of the official state religion, the Church of England. Although this was a Protestant church, it was still influenced by Catholic rituals. A lot of people, including many members of Parliament, disliked the Church of England and longed for a very simple, basic form of worship. They were known in England as Puritans.

Charles believed in the 'divine right of kings'. This meant that he believed that God had given him, rather than Parliament, the right to rule his people. Many members of Parliament did not like this, and nor did they like Charles's extravagant demands for money. They often

Charles and Cromwell

Charles I (1600–1649) was a small, shy man who had not expected to be king. He had an elder brother who died young. He was good-natured and honourable, but so lacked confidence that he was hopeless at dealing with people, and was very easily influenced by those who loved or flattered him. He really believed that he was king by God's wish, and this made him behave thoughtlessly towards those he ruled, insisting on having his own way. This annoyed some people, but many loved him and were loyal to him.

Oliver Cromwell (1599–1658) was a member of Parliament who turned out to be a great general, organizing the Parliamentarians into an efficient fighting force called 'The New Model Army'. After the king was executed in 1649, England became a 'Commonwealth' (republic). In 1653 Cromwell dissolved Parliament and ruled alone as 'Lord Protector'. He became very unpopular. He was so extreme a Puritan that he made all forms of fun and entertainment illegal, even the wearing of bright colours! He died in 1658, and two years later Charles's son was asked to take the throne as King Charles II.

complained about royal spending, and refused his demands to raise new taxes. They also did not like or trust Charles's chief minister, the Duke of Buckingham. Charles was angry at this and unwisely dismissed Parliament. In 1628 Buckingham was murdered. Charles now turned to his wife, Queen Henrietta Maria, as adviser. This was even worse, for she was Catholic, and the English would never again accept Catholicism as the state religion.

The Outbreak of War

In the 'Eleven Years' Tyranny' that followed, Charles ruled without Parliament. During this period Charles tried to get the people of Scotland to accept bishops in their church. In 1638 many Scots signed a 'Covenant' (promise) never to accept bishops, and in 1640 the Scottish Covenanters invaded England. This crisis forced Charles to summon Parliament again, in order to raise more money to fight the Scots. Parliament then introduced many

A lively Representation of the manner how his late Majesty was beheaded uppon the Scaffold Ian:30:1648:

The Death of King Charles I

Charles I was calm and dignified at his execution. He wore two shirts so that he would not shiver from cold (it was January) and seem afraid. He asked for his beard not to be cut off, as it had done no harm.

Major battles of the Civil War.

measures to limit the king's power. In 1642 Charles tried to arrest five members of Parliament, and shortly afterwards civil war broke out between the two sides.

The war continued on and off for seven years. Sometimes members of one family took different sides. There were many battles, but in the end the Parliamentarians, under their leader Oliver Cromwell, were victorious. In 1649 Charles was tried and executed.

Conflict in Ireland

The Battle of the Boyne, 1690, saw the defeat of the Catholic James II by the Protestant army of William of Orange (William III).

The English began a conquest of Ireland in the 12th century when English knights took Irish land and settled there. However, Irish chieftains continued to rule large areas of Ireland. Up until the 16th century the only part of Ireland ruled effectively by England was an area around Dublin, known as the Irish Pale.

King Henry VIII of England (ruled 1509–1547) forced Irish leaders to recognize him as their overlord. In return they were given English titles, such as 'earl'. England and Ireland were Catholic countries until Henry VIII broke ties with the Roman Catholic Church in 1534. England then became a Protestant country, and Henry also outlawed the Catholic religion in Ireland. However, the Irish ignored the law and Ireland remained Catholic.

Henry's successors decided to increase English influence in Ireland. Parts of Ireland were colonized by English people and many Irish

The Battle of the Boyne

When a Catholic, James II, became king of England in 1685 the Irish thought he might give them back their lands. However, the English overthrew their Catholic king in 1688 and replaced him with a Dutch Protestant, William of Orange. James arrived in Ireland in 1689 with a French army to join the Irish, who agreed to help him reclaim the English throne. In 1689 William of Orange arrived in Ireland with an army to fight James. A fierce battle took place at the River Boyne in 1690, and James was defeated and fled to France. The Irish and French continued fighting, but surrendered after a defeat at Limerick.

were driven from their homes. Irish rebellions against English rule were put down brutally. After one rebellion Queen Elizabeth I (ruled 1558–1603) sent an English army to Ireland that killed thousands of Irish people and destroyed villages, crops, and cattle.

The Flight of the Earls

In 1607 the English suspected that the earls of Tyrconnell and Tyrone were plotting a new rebellion. The earls, thinking they were going to be arrested, left Ireland for Italy – an event known as 'the flight of the earls'. Their lands, which were in Ulster, a large region in the north of Ireland, were seized and Protestant settlers from England and Scotland moved there. Over the next century thousands of English settlers were given Irish land so that by the end of the 17th century the Irish owned only about one-tenth of the land in their own country.

The Rebellion of 1641–1649

In 1641 the Irish began a series of uprisings to drive out the English. Over the years they became angrier and angrier about the loss of their lands. They also suffered English laws that forbade them to practise their religion, play Irish music, or speak Gaelic, their native language. The rebellion started in Ulster – where the Irish attacked and killed large numbers of Protestant settlers – and continued for eight years.

In 1649 the English general Oliver Cromwell, who had led the Parliamentarians to victory against King Charles I in the English Civil War, entered Ireland with a large army to end Irish

The Treaty of Limerick

In 1691 the Treaty of Limerick was signed after the Irish surrendered to William of Orange. In the treaty certain promises were made to the Irish soldiers, including allowing the Irish to remain Catholic and returning some of their land. However, the English broke the terms of the treaty. Thousands of Irish soldiers left for France, where they founded an army called the Irish Brigade. They fought for France in many battles and won fame for their bravery. Their battle cry was 'Remember Limerick', referring to the broken treaty.

English forces led by William III defeated the Irish at Limerick in 1691.

resistance for good. His brutal actions, in which thousands were massacred, struck fear into the Irish people. He laid siege to Irish fortresses, including one in Drogheda, where all the soldiers and many of the townspeople were slaughtered. Before Cromwell returned to England he forced the Irish from huge areas of land and divided the territories between his soldiers and supporters.

Scotland

Border Wars

The Scots had fought off a number of English attempts to conquer their country but there was almost continuous warfare between the two countries for the next 300 years. Border raiders (called reivers) constantly stole cattle and burnt farms and villages on both sides of the border, and there were many battles between the English and Scottish armies.

For many years Scotland had a series of kings who were quite weak and nobles who were powerful and challenged the king's rule. There were constant plots and threats. King James I (ruled 1406–1437), who raised taxes, was stabbed to death in 1437 by a group of these rebel nobles. Meanwhile, violent feuds went on between different clans (families).

When Queen Elizabeth I of England died in 1603, the English throne passed to her distant relative James VI of Scotland, who became James I of England. For a century the monarchs of Scotland were also monarchs of England, but both countries had separate parliaments. Then in 1707 the Scottish parliament was abolished, and the kingdoms Scotland and England were joined as the United Kingdom of Great Britain.

Mary, Queen of Scots (ruled 1542–1587)

Mary Stuart, who was called the Queen of Scots, was born in 1542 and became queen only a week later when her father, King James V of Scotland, died. The English wanted Mary to marry Henry VIII's son Edward, and sent armies to Scotland to persuade the Scots to agree. The Scots disliked this 'rough wooing', and sent the five-year-old Mary to France for safety. There Mary married the future king of France, called the Dauphin, when she was 15 years old and he was only 14. However, he died two years later, and Mary came back to Scotland.

Although Scotland was a Protestant country, Mary was Catholic, and she was not popular with the Scottish nobles. She married her cousin, Lord Darnley, and they had one son, who later became James I of England. In 1567, however, Darnley was murdered.

Shortly afterwards Mary married the Earl of Bothwell, who was one of those responsible for the murder. Many people thought Mary too was involved, and she was forced to give up her throne and flee to England. She hoped that Queen Elizabeth I would protect her, but instead she was locked up for nearly 20 years. Elizabeth suspected that Mary plotted to become queen of England, and finally had her beheaded in 1587 for treason.

The massacre of the McDonalds by the Campbells at Glencoe in February 1692.

The Covenanters

In 1560, John Knox brought the ideas of the Protestant Reformation to Scotland. Reformers wanted to rid the church of anything Roman Catholic. They formed the Church of Scotland, which is Presbyterian (ruled by elected elders), instead of Episcopalian (ruled by bishops) like the Church of England. Some old churches were destroyed by mobs because they were reminders of Catholic ways.

In 1637 King Charles I tried to make the Scots use the English Prayer Book, but they rebelled against this and formed an army to fight him. Charles didn't have the money to fight a war and he finally made peace with Scotland four years later. Many Scots signed covenants, which were agreements about ways of worshipping as well as how the country was to be ruled. Some even signed the first covenant (1638) in blood. Thousands of these Covenanters were killed in religious struggles between 1661 and 1688, and at one point 300 ministers were thrown out of their parishes. Eventually, however, the Scots were allowed to keep their own form of religion.

The Massacre of Glencoe

Many people in Lowland Scotland feared the Gaelic-speaking Highland clans, whom they thought of as warlike and lawless. The government decided to kill all the members of one clan to scare the other clans and to warn them not to support the Jacobites – people who wanted the Catholic King James VII, who was in exile, to be restored to the throne. When a chief of the Macdonald clan accidentally arrived six days late for swearing an oath of loyalty to King William (the Protestant king who had replaced James on the throne), he was said to be guilty of treason. In the early morning of 13 February 1692 a group of government soldiers staying in Glencoe murdered 38 of their Macdonald hosts. The government soldiers were mostly Campbells, old enemies of the Macdonalds, and the massacre caused much anger and hatred towards the government.

The Thirty Years' War

From 1618 to 1648 a series of conflicts known as the Thirty Years' War ravaged Europe. The war began as a religious conflict between Catholics and Protestants in the Holy Roman Empire. This empire, which was ruled by the Austrian Habsburg family, covered much of central and western Europe.

The Defenestration of Prague

The Habsburgs followed the Catholic religion, but many states within their empire followed the Protestant religion. In 1618 King Ferdinand of Bohemia and Hungary, a Habsburg, tried to make all the people he ruled follow the Catholic religion. This caused a great deal of anger among the Protestants, and the Protestant nobles in his kingdom rebelled. In the Bohemian capital of Prague, Protestants invaded the royal palace and threw two of Ferdinand's officials out of a window. This act became known as the Defenestration of Prague (defenestration is from the Latin word *fenestra,* which means 'window').

In 1619 Ferdinand was crowned Holy Roman Emperor. That same year the rebellious Protestants elected Frederick V as the new king of Bohemia. With the support of Spain, Poland, and Bavaria Ferdinand gathered together an army to crush the Bohemian rebels.

The Protestant army was defeated at the Battle of the White Mountain, near Prague, in 1620 and Frederick was overthrown. Ferdinand then forced the Protestants of Bohemia to become Catholic.

Two imperial officials were thrown from a window in Prague castle by Protestants in 1618.

Other Countries Enter the War

Other countries in Europe were drawn into the fighting. Catholic Spanish troops fought in Germany, Italy, and France. The Dutch sent money to help Frederick's generals and Christian IV of Denmark, who feared Ferdinand's armies. In 1626 Christian's forces were defeated in battle. Ferdinand declared that

The Battle of the White Mountain in Bohemia in 1620 was a defeat for the Protestant forces.

all property taken by the Protestants since 1552 was to be restored to the Catholic church. However, after Denmark withdrew, Protestant Sweden, encouraged by France, joined in. The Swedish king Gustavus II Adolphus landed in Pomerania in 1630 to begin a series of successful campaigns against Ferdinand's armies, including the Battle of Breitenfeld in 1631.

After Gustavus Adolphus's death France, although Catholic, declared war on Spain in 1635, in alliance with Sweden and some German Protestant princes. In 1640 Catalonia and Portugal rebelled against Spain, even though all three were Catholic.

The End of the War

In 1648 the Peace of Westphalia brought an end to the conflict between France, Sweden, the Holy Roman emperor, and the German princes,

battle
majority of people Catholic
majority of people Protestant

although other wars carried on for some years longer. The Habsburgs had failed to strengthen the empire and in fact lost many powers. The German princes had won the right to choose their religion. Sweden had become the dominant power in the Baltic, and France had become the dominant power in western Europe.

War and Weapons

There were wars going on in Europe almost constantly as countries tried to expand their territory and settled their arguments by force. Wars were also fought over religious differences, especially after the Protestants broke away from the Roman Catholic Church in the 16th century. Huge amounts of money were needed to pay for these wars, which might not come to an end until the rulers went bankrupt. Kings and lords often led their troops in battle, and their sons trained as knights so that they could serve in their armies.

Siege Warfare

An old way of taking control of a city or castle was to surround it with soldiers and try to break in. Ladders and giant towers were wheeled up to the walls, archers shot arrows, catapults hurled stones, and battering rams (long wooden beams with metal tips) tried to break down the gates. If none of this was successful, sieges could last for as long as a year. No food would be allowed into the city and wells might be poisoned, so in the end the people inside had to give up or starve. When cannon that could blast through stone walls appeared, castles were no longer so useful for defence.

An aerial view of Deal Castle in Kent, built by Henry VIII in 1539 as part of England's coastal defences.

Armour

In the Middle Ages knights wore chain mail, which was made from linked iron rings, but by the 15th century many had full suits of armour made of plates of steel. These provided better protection, but were extremely heavy and uncomfortable to wear, less flexible than chain mail, and very expensive. Horses would also wear armour in battles. As guns improved, armour was less effective and simply slowed down the soldiers. From around the middle of the 17th century many soldiers only wore a helmet and breastplate, and by the end of the 17th century few soldiers wore any armour at all.

Two German soldiers of the Thirty Years' War. The man on the left carries a musket.

Woes of War

Horrible injuries happened in wars, and sometimes the only treatment for a wound was to amputate (cut off) an arm or leg. But illness caused even more deaths than battle wounds. Many troops were not paid enough to live on, so they raided villages for food, sometimes even burning the houses of peasants. Ongoing wars made life miserable for ordinary people, many of whom died of starvation or disease.

Early Armies

In Europe before 1600 many soldiers were mercenaries – they would fight for whoever paid them the most. Other soldiers were ordinary peasants who had to fight if there was a war. Most armies were poorly trained and undisciplined, with no real uniform. They had to live in bad conditions without being properly paid or fed, so they would often get what they needed by stealing and plundering.

Governments began to realize that they would be better off training professional soldiers in a regular army rather than expecting civilians or mercenaries to fight for them. In the English Civil War, Parliament set up a 'New Model Army' with trained men who worked full time for wages. Being a soldier became a proper job.

Weapons of War

Longbows, invented in the 13th century, helped England win the battle of Agincourt in 1415. A longbow was 2 metres (6½ feet) tall and its arrows could pierce through plate armour. The first guns in Europe were used in the early 15th century. They were tubes of metal mounted on long wooden shafts. Over the next three

A 16th-century painting of a battle at sea.

centuries a whole range of hand-held guns and cannons were developed, but these early devices were dangerous to use, and could injure the people using them. In 1460 King James II of Scotland was killed when one of his own cannons exploded. In the 17th century new and improved firearms were introduced. The flintlock pistol had a safer firing mechanism, and a flintlock musket was invented with a bayonet (knife) attached to the end. Lighter cannons, mounted on two wheels, made it easier to move artillery around during a battle.

Naval battles were fought at close range. At first the gunners were raised up on 'castles' attached to the deck. From this position they tried to blast through the rigging and hull of the enemy ship with pistols, small cannon, brass grenades, and even rocks. Later, bigger guns were mounted along both sides of the ship, below the top deck. Grappling hooks were used to pull an enemy ship alongside, and sailors armed with swords, battle axes, pistols, and pikes would board the enemy ship and fight hand-to-hand.

Absolute Rulers of Europe

Absolutism is a system of government where one person, or a group of people, rules with unlimited power. Traditionally it was believed that absolute monarchs got their authority from God, a system known as 'the divine right of kings'. This meant they did not have to answer to any earthly government and could do as they wished.

Absolute monarchs ruled ancient Egypt, Rome, and China. Modern absolutism began in the 16th century when individual nations began to develop in Europe. Countries with absolute monarchs included England, France, Spain, and Austria.

Louis XIV

King Louis XIV of France (ruled 1643–1715) is one of the best examples of an absolute monarch. He became king in 1643 when he was only four years old. A civil war broke out in 1648 when French nobles and ministers rose against the king. Louis suffered hunger, fear, and humiliation during this war. The conflict lasted

Louis XIV took absolute control of the government of France in 1661.

The Palace at Versailles

Louis XIV's love of grandeur can be seen in the magnificent palace he had built at Versailles, just outside Paris. In 1682 Louis moved his government there, although the palace was originally built as a place for pleasure. Great writers and artists stayed at Versailles, and paintings and sculptures by French masters adorned the luxurious rooms. About 5,000 servants lived in the palace and about 14,000 servants and soldiers lived nearby. The enormous cost of building and running Versailles is partly why France became almost bankrupt during Louis's reign.

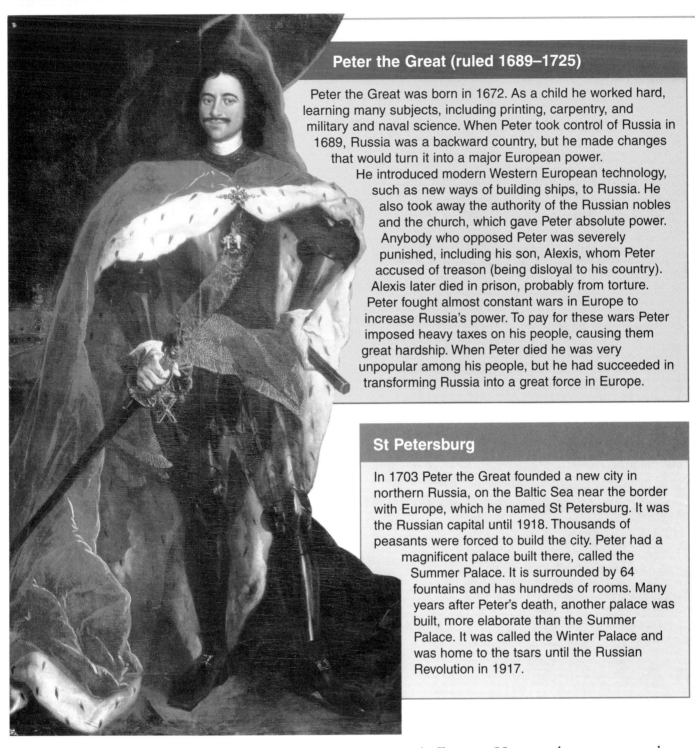

Peter the Great (ruled 1689–1725)

Peter the Great was born in 1672. As a child he worked hard, learning many subjects, including printing, carpentry, and military and naval science. When Peter took control of Russia in 1689, Russia was a backward country, but he made changes that would turn it into a major European power.

He introduced modern Western European technology, such as new ways of building ships, to Russia. He also took away the authority of the Russian nobles and the church, which gave Peter absolute power. Anybody who opposed Peter was severely punished, including his son, Alexis, whom Peter accused of treason (being disloyal to his country). Alexis later died in prison, probably from torture. Peter fought almost constant wars in Europe to increase Russia's power. To pay for these wars Peter imposed heavy taxes on his people, causing them great hardship. When Peter died he was very unpopular among his people, but he had succeeded in transforming Russia into a great force in Europe.

St Petersburg

In 1703 Peter the Great founded a new city in northern Russia, on the Baltic Sea near the border with Europe, which he named St Petersburg. It was the Russian capital until 1918. Thousands of peasants were forced to build the city. Peter had a magnificent palace built there, called the Summer Palace. It is surrounded by 64 fountains and has hundreds of rooms. Many years after Peter's death, another palace was built, more elaborate than the Summer Palace. It was called the Winter Palace and was home to the tsars until the Russian Revolution in 1917.

until 1653, when the rebellion was crushed. This frightening period of the young king's life is possibly why Louis decided to become an absolute monarch. When the French chief minister died in 1661, Louis announced to the other ministers that he would become his own chief minister and take control of the whole government.

Louis was very ambitious and wanted France to become the most magnificent and powerful country in Europe. He was almost constantly at war with other European countries, which formed alliances to limit France's growing power. Over the years these wars, together with Louis's love of extravagant living, cost France dearly. Louis showed little interest in his people, who suffered great hardship, and at his death in 1715 France was nearly bankrupt. He was an unpopular king, and at his funeral people jeered as his coffin was transported through the streets of Paris.

Society Divided

For hundreds of years the countries of Europe had been run on a feudal system. This meant that only a few very rich people owned most of the land, and almost all the others worked for them, practically as slaves. Gradually, this was changing. Some peasants were able to buy their freedom and set up as craftspeople in towns and villages. Others, yeomen, were able to buy up more land to farm for themselves and even pay workmen to help them in their fields. They could then afford to live in better houses, and perhaps send their children to school.

Wat Tyler and John Ball lead the Peasants' Revolt to London to make their demands heard.

Peasant workers are shown harvesting grapes near the Château de Saumur in this 15th-century illustration.

Money, Land, and Power

The upper classes were the nobles and gentry – the most important people after the king. They lived in grand manor houses with many servants, and because they owned the land, they had power over the poor in their villages. Around the 17th century, however, some merchants had begun to get so rich that they became more powerful than many nobles. Some merchants owned ships that brought valuable products from all over the world to Europe; they controlled buying, selling, and transport, and had workshops where goods were made. Some successful merchants became bankers, and kings and nobles borrowed money from them.

Wat Tyler is killed by William Walworth, the mayor of London. After this the Peasants' Revolt collapsed.

Peasants' Revolts

The poor did not always suffer in silence. Some of them rebelled against the unfair rules. There were a number of uprisings by peasants and other workers throughout the 14th century in Flanders (modern Belgium), France, Italy, and England.

In England, a priest from York called John Ball travelled around the country, saying that God created people to be equals. In 1381 he and Wat Tyler led a group of 60,000 labourers from Essex and Kent to London to demand an end to serfdom (the system under which many peasants were treated like slaves), the unfair poll tax, and high rents. At first the protesters were peaceful, but then they got out of control and beheaded the chancellor (who was also archbishop of Canterbury) and the treasurer, whom they blamed for the poll tax. At a later meeting with the king the mayor of London cut down Wat Tyler with his sword, and Tyler was dragged away and beheaded. The young King Richard II met the rebels and made a promise to help the peasants, but he did not keep it. Later, John Ball and many others were hanged for encouraging the peasants to rebel.

Popular uprisings continued in Europe. In 1524 and 1525, 100,000 peasants were killed in the Peasants' War in Germany. In most cases the groups of peasants had little military power or organization and were easily crushed.

The Suffering of the Poor

Most peasants' lives were short and hard. Unfair taxes and laws made life even more difficult, and many people had only just enough food to live on. Some had a little land for themselves, where they could grow their own food. But others were even poorer, and had no land. They had to go out each day and find work on someone else's farm.

After many people died from the Black Death in the mid-14th century, things changed for the better for some of the peasants who survived. There were not enough labourers to do all the work, so they could ask for higher wages. In Britain the government passed a law to stop this.

Poor people who were too old or weak to work for a living, or could not get jobs, might be forced to beg for food and clothing. During years of very bad harvests, many people would take to the road, desperate to find food. Often the church provided some help, or built almshouses for old people to live in (the word 'alms' means a gift of charity). However, if beggars were thought to be just lazy, they would be whipped or put into workhouses, which were like prisons.

Clergy Class

Churchmen, such as priests, bishops, and monks, belonged to the clergy class. The church was powerful and owned a lot of land. Some churchmen grew very wealthy and were given special privileges. In France, only the poor peasants paid taxes – the clergy and nobility did not have to, even though they had far more money. The government executed people who protested against this.

Food and Farms

Peasant farmers worked from dawn to dusk, six days a week. They ploughed the land, sowed the seeds, and reaped the harvest with only the most basic of tools. Because they had to pay for their own small plots of land by doing extra work for the landowners, peasants ended up with little to live on. From 1600 to 1720 the weather was so cold in Europe that it has been called the Little Ice Age. Crops did badly and many poor farmers starved.

An aerial view of the church and village of Lyddington. Ploughed fields can be seen in the background.

Bread, made of coarse rye or oat flour, was the main food for the poor. Water was not very safe to drink so grown-ups and children drank beer, cider, or perry, a kind of cider made from pears. Another common food was pottage, a thick soup. For the poor, bacon, fish, eggs, and cheese would be occasional luxuries. The noonday meal was often eaten in the fields.

Wealthy people drank wine with their meals. They held feasts with many courses, and the meal could last for hours. Even at elegant meals, only knives and spoons were used at the table, until forks became more common in the 17th century. People used their fingers to eat and washed their hands before and after the meal.

Although people ate an amazing variety of meat (even songbirds like larks and blackbirds!), only poor people ate many vegetables at this time in Europe. However, by the 17th century more fruit and vegetables were being grown in gardens, and recipe books were being published with new dishes from foreign countries.

The Cottage Garden

For ordinary people, every bit of land they owned had to be put to good use to provide food. Instead of having a grassy lawn and flower beds, they grew vegetables like parsnips, carrots, cabbages, turnips, pumpkins, and herbs. Many people kept a cow, chickens, or a pig. Beehives were set up to provide honey and candle wax. Because there was not enough fodder to keep animals through the winter, they were often killed in the autumn and the meat was salted, smoked, or dried to keep it from going bad.

New Ways of Farming

In England, land was split up into long, narrow strips to divide the land more evenly among the peasants. As well as growing barley, rye, oats, wheat, and peas on their own strips, the peasants could gather firewood or let animals graze on common land around the village.

As the population of Europe grew larger, more land was needed for food and fuel. Big landowners started getting more fields for themselves by enclosure, surrounding the land they wanted with hedges or ditches to keep other people off. This meant that they were taking away the common ground and

sometimes even the tenants' fields. The landowners had more room to graze their sheep and grow their crops, but the peasants ended up with even less then they had before.

Some parts of Europe were so low lying that every so often they were flooded by the sea. In the Netherlands, people got very good at draining the sea and building dykes (stone walls) to keep the water back so that they could grow their crops. They also used windmills to pump the seawater away, and reclaimed many acres of fertile land.

Labourers are shown at work on a farm in spring in this 16th-century Flemish painting.

Work and Trades

During the Middle Ages and later, almost everything was made and repaired by hand, with simple tools. This made some goods very expensive, such as shoes and clothes, which were made to measure and took many hours to produce.

Crafts of the time show us how people lived. Saddlers, who made and fixed harnesses and saddles, were important because horses were the main kind of transport. Wheelwrights made wheels for carts and coaches. Carpenters made the wooden framework of houses, furniture, and ships, and even machinery in windmills and watermills. Better mills were now used to grind corn, shrink cloth, and make paper.

A woman sits spinning at the door of her cottage watching as hunters pass by.

Cottage Industries

Many people worked in their own homes, especially if they were involved in the wool trade, which was very important in Europe, especially England. The spinning of thread was usually done by women and children, but men did the weaving, and then other skilled workers would dye and finish the cloth. Middlemen took the cloth to merchants who were able to sell it for much more than the weavers were paid. Flax (for linen) and silk were also used for clothmaking, and by the end of the 17th century, cotton was coming into Europe.

Most children worked alongside their parents, helping with household chores and perhaps learning the family trade. They might be sent away to train as servants for wealthier families when they were 11 or 12.

Skilled artists engraving metal plates that might be used to make illustrations for books.

Town Trades

Town streets were often crowded with porters carrying bundles (many streets were too narrow for carts), water carriers, sweeps, pie sellers, rat catchers, even peddlers selling song-sheets of popular ballads. A knife grinder worked in the street, and the town crier shouted out news. A blacksmith's forge was in a workshop at the end of his house, and bakers displayed bread on their window ledges. Many traders would take a stall in the town market once a week, and would perhaps produce fancier goods for yearly fairs.

Tradespeople all had to belong to guilds, organizations that collected money from members and made sure that everyone's work was good enough. They also checked the training of apprentices. Three quarters of England's foreign trade was controlled by a trading company called the Merchant Adventurers in the mid-16th century.

The city of Venice was a great centre of trade from the 13th to the 19th centuries.

Sports and Games

Festival Fun

The main times most people had to relax in England were Sundays, holy days (which became known as holidays), and religious festivals. Fairs were often held on feast days and holy days such as Easter. At these fairs there were religious plays and jugglers and acrobats in the streets, as well as things for sale. During the Twelve Days of Christmas, people paraded in masks and extravagant costumes, and actors called mummers performed plays in mime.

Celebrations on the first of May meant another day off work for most people. A tall tree was cut down for a maypole and decorated with leaves and flowers. The May King and Queen were chosen, and there would be dancing on the village green.

The winters of the late 17th century were sometimes so cold that 'frost fairs' were held on the River Thames. The ice was so thick that fires could be lit on it! People used skates with wooden blades to travel over the ice.

Games on the Green

Contests of wrestling, running, jumping, and throwing the hammer were often held on village greens. In the game called pall-mall, players had to hit a wooden ball through a hanging iron ring with a stick like a croquet mallet. Archery was encouraged because it was good practice for using the longbow in wartime.

A 'frost fair' held on the frozen River Thames during the winter of 1683.

Sailors' Pastimes

To liven up long months at sea, sailors would gamble with dice or cards, and listen to storytellers 'spin yarns' (tell tall stories). Board games such as Nine-Man's Morris, backgammon, chess, or draughts were also played on board ship. Sailors sang folk songs and ballads, and danced to the music of lutes, pipes, or a drum called the tabor.

A 16th-century painting by Pieter Brueghel showing a variety of children's games.

Child's Play

Many of the games played by children, such as leap-frog, tag, and follow-my-leader are still known today. In Tudor times, swings, stilts, skittles, and hoops were common playthings, and richer children played with dolls, toy guns, and rocking horses.

New Games

'Real' (meaning 'royal') tennis became popular in France in the 15th century, and was played indoors, with a rope in place of a net. Another new game for wealthy people was billiards. Golf, played with a wooden ball, also appeared, but at first it was called a 'game for idlers'! Later, rules were set by golfers in St Andrews, Scotland. Cricket had become very popular in England by 1700. During the time when Oliver Cromwell was Lord Protector of England, however, the Puritans outlawed games. Most people were not happy about this.

Going for Blood

Many of the games and sports of Tudor and Stuart times seem brutal to us now. In cudgel play, each competitor tried to whack the other over the head with a heavy wooden club! Football was often played on Sundays with a blown-up pig's bladder for a ball. Hundreds of people might play the same game at the same time. It was such a rough game that many players had their arms or legs broken, and the town constable stood by to break up fights. In England the government often tried to ban football, as it kept young men from their archery practice.

Crowds flocked to see animal fights and bet money on which animal they thought would win. London had many cockpits, where two cocks with sharp spurs attached to their legs fought each other to the death. Bear-baiting often took place in fenced-in bear gardens. A bear (or sometimes a bull or wild boar) was chained to a post and tried to defend itself while angry, snapping dogs were set on it.

Kings and their courts loved to hunt stags, wild boar, and wolves on horseback, and they often held a lavish ball or masque after the hunt. Nobles might fight each other in sword duels, which could end in death or serious injury. In the 15th century, however, duelling was banned by law.

Index

Picture Acknowledgements

t = top, b = bottom, l = left, r = right

4 Erich Lessing/AKG London; 5 K Gillham/Robert Harding; 6 t AKG London, b Kozu Collection, Kyoto/Werner Forman Archive; 7 Christie's Images; 8 Corbis; 9 t Christie's Images, 9 b–10 t Werner Forman Archive; 10 b AKG London; 11 Werner Forman Archive; 12 Palazzo Ducale, Venice/Bridgeman Art Library; 13 t Victoria & Albert Museum/et archive, b Erich Lessing/AKG London; 14 Erich Lessing/ AKG London; 15 et archive; 16 James Davis Travel Photography; 17 et archive; 18 t Archives Nationales, Paris/AKG London, b et archive; 19 Bibliothèque Nationale, Paris/et archive; 20 t National Museum, Copenhagen/Bridgeman Art Library, b David King; 21 AKG London; 22 t et archive; 22 bl & br Annette Godefroid/AKG London; 23 et archive; 24 t Museo e Arte Antiga, Lisbon/et archive, b Pierpoint Morgan Library, New York/AKG London; 25 D M Halford; 26 l Jean-Louis Nou/AKG London, r AKG London; 27 AKG London; 28 Corbis; 28–29 Paul Thompson/Eye Ubiquitous; 29 Mary Evans Picture Library; 30 AKG London; 31 l New York Public Library/AKG London, r AKG London; 32 et archive; 33 t Private collection/Bridgeman Art Library, b National Gallery of Victoria, Melbourne/ Bridgeman Art Library; 34 t British Museum/et archive, b Christie's Images; 35–36 AKG London; 37 British Library/et archive; 39 t et archive, b Private Collection/Michael Graham-Stewart/Bridgeman Art Library; 40 r Sammlung Godefroie, Hamburg/AKG London; l AKG London; 41 t Galeria degli Uffizi/Bridgeman Art Library, b AKG London; 42 l Galleria degli Uffizi/Bridgeman Art Library, r Museo del Bargello, Florence/et archive; 43 t Galeria degli Uffizi, Florence/AKG London; b Vatican Museums and Galleries/Bridgeman Art Library; 44 t Correr Museum, Venice/et archive, b AKG London; 45 t Phillips, The International Fine Art Auctioneers, UK/Bridgeman Art Library, b British Museum/et archive; 46 et archive; 47 l Science Museum/Science and Society Picture Library, r AKG London; 48 t Civic Museum, Colmar/et archive, b AKG London; 49 British Library/et archive; 50 Museum of London/et archive; 50–51 Museum of Fine Art, Budapest, Hungary/Bridgeman Art Library; 52 t Mary Evans Picture Library, b Bibliothèque Nationale, Paris/AKG London; 53 Mary Evans Picture Library; 54 t Museum der Stadt, Regensburg/AKG London, b Bible Society, UK/Bridgeman Art Library; 55 Collection of Albert Rilliet, Switzerland/Lauros-Giraudon/Bridgeman Art Library; 56 t Phillips, The International Fine Art Auctioneers, UK/Bridgeman Art Library, b Kunsthistorisches Museum, Vienna/ Erich Lessing/AKG London; 57 Museo del Prado, Madrid/AKG London; 58 t Private Collection/ Bridgeman Art Library, b British Library/et archive; 59 et archive; 60 Erich Lessing/AKG London; 61 l AKG London, r Stationers' Hall, UK/Bridgeman Art Library; 63 t Private Collection/Bridgeman Art Library, b Philips, The International Fine Art Auctioneers, UK Bridgeman Art Library; 64 Belvoir Castle, Leicestershire, UK/Bridgeman Art Library; 65 t Kunsthistorisches Museum, Vienna/Bridgeman Art Library, b Skyscan Photolibrary; 66 t Christie's Images, b et archive; 67 Woburn Abbey, UK/Bridgeman Art Library; 68 Kunsthistorisches Museum, Vienna/Bridgeman Art Library; 69 AKG London; 70 Philip Mould, Historical Portraits Ltd, London/Bridgeman Art Library; 71 et archive; 72 JA Brooks/Jarrold/et archive; 73 National Army Museum/et archive; 74 Versailles/et archive; 75 Mary Evans Picture Library; 77 t AKG London, b Erich Lessing/AKG London; 78 t Skyscan Photolibrary, b AKG London; 79 National Maritime Museum, London; 80 t Musée du Louvre, Paris/Erich Lessing/AKG London, b AKG London; 81 Hermitage Museum, St Petersburg/AKG London; 82 t British Library, London/ Bridgeman Art Library, b Musée Conde, Chantilly/AKG London; 83 British Library, London/Bridgeman Art Library; 84 Skyscan Photolibrary; 85 l Musée des Beaux Arts, Lille/et archive, r Geoff Kidd/Oxford Scientific Films; 86 t Mary Evans Picture Library, b Stapleton Collection, UK/Bridgeman Art Library; 87 et archive; 88 Museum of London, UK/Bridgeman Art Library; 89 AKG London.

Cover illustrations (clockwise from top right):
Galleria degli Uffizi, Florence/AKG London; Sammlung Godefroid, Hamburg/AKG London; AKG London; AKG London; Corbis

Every effort has been made to give the correct acknowledgement for each picture. However, should there be any inaccuracy or omission, we would be pleased to insert the correct acknowledgement in a future edition or printing of this volume.